# A
# CONVERSATION
## with
# ANNE DAMMARELL

# A
# CONVERSATION
## with
# ANNE DAMMARELL

*Interviewed by: Charles Stuart Kennedy*
*Initial Session: June 10th, 2013*

*Diplomatic Oral History Series*
*Association for Diplomatic Studies and Training*

# ANNE DAMMARELL

CITI OF
BOOKS

**CITIOFBOOKS, INC.**
3736 Eubank NE Suite A1
Albuquerque, NM 87111-3579
*www.citiofbooks.com*
Hotline:            1 (877) 389-2759
Fax:                1 (505) 930-7244

Ordering Information:

Quantity sales. Special discounts are available on quantity purchases by corporations, associations, and others. For details, contact the publisher at the address above.

Printed in the United States of America.

ISBN-13:       Softcover            979-8-89391-302-6

               eBook                979-8-89391-303-3

Library of Congress Control Number: 2024917968

# CONTENTS

Dedicated to all my nieces and nephews, especially
Annie Fitzpatrick,
Kathy Dammarell Magistrelli,
and
Tara Simon,
who made 1983 a happy time.

# FOREWORD

## The ADST Diplomatic Oral History Series

For over 235 years extraordinary diplomats have served the United States at home and abroad with courage and dedication. Yet their accomplishments in promoting and protecting American interests usually remain little known to their compatriots. The Association for Diplomatic Studies and Training (ADST) created the Diplomatic Oral History Series to help fill this void by publishing in book form selected transcripts of interviews from its Foreign Affairs Oral History Collection.

The text contained herein acquaints readers with the life of Anne Dammarell and her rewarding, challenging, and even dangerous career as an officer for the United States Agency for International Development. We are proud to make her interview available through the Diplomatic Oral History Series.

ADST (www.adst.org) is an independent nonprofit organization founded in 1986 and committed to supporting training of foreign affairs personnel at the State Department's Foreign Service Institute and advancing knowledge of American diplomacy. It places the transcripts of the Foreign Affairs Oral History collection on its website and the site of the Library of Congress.

ADST also sponsors books on diplomacy through its Memoirs and Occasional Papers Series and, jointly with DACOR (an organization of foreign affairs professionals), the Diplomats and Diplomacy Series. ADST manages an educational website at www.usdiplomacy.org.

*Kenneth L. Brown*
*President, ADST*

# ORIGINS

*Q: You go by Anne, I think.*

DAMMARELL: I do.

*Q: OK, Anne, let's start at the beginning. When and where were you born?*

DAMMARELL: I was born January 2, 1938 in Cincinnati, Ohio.

*Q: Please talk about your father's side of the family, and then we'll do your mother's side. What do you know about the Dammarells?*

DAMMARELL: Well, I know a fair amount. The name Dammarell is unusual. It's an anglicized French name. You don't come across many of them in this country. Both my father and his father were interested in family history.

*Q: Yes.*

DAMMARELL: They come from the southern part of England. My great grandfather, William Dammarell, was born in England. His parents left Devon for Prince Edward Island, Canada when he was a little boy. I'm sure it was an economic need, no question about it. I was told they were ship chandlers. I've been to Prince Edward Island and have seen the family tombstones. It appears that the women stayed, married, and died there. They had their maiden and married names listed. I found that interesting. I think all the boys left. My grandfather left in his late teens.

*Q: I haven't followed through, but in my family tradition my grandfather came from there too.*

DAMMARELL: From the southern part of England?

*Q: No, from Prince Edward Island.*

DAMMARELL: Yes, many English landed in Prince Edward Island in the nineteenth century. My great grandfather left PEI as a teenager. Why he went to Cincinnati, I do not know, because there were no Dammarells there. It could have been the waterways.

*Q: Yes, could have been. Going down that way would be part of the flow of migration, you might say. What did he do?*

DAMMARELL: He was a tinner, a roofer. Roofers were called tinners. My father remembered him. I have pictures of him. He married an Irish woman, Annie Brennan. They had several children. Their only surviving son, Luke, was my grandfather.

*Q: Well, let's talk about your grandmother.*

DAMMARELL: My great grandmother?

*Q: Yes, great.*

DAMMARELL: I did not know much about my great grandmother, Annie Brennan. She was Roman Catholic and my great grandfather, of course, was Protestant. He became a Roman Catholic late in life. When my father was in his early twenties he visited his dying grandfather. He wanted to find out why his grandfather had changed religion. He thought he was going to get some religious insight. His grandfather just looked at him and said, "I don't know; I just liked going to that church." There is a nice little story about him that shows he must have been a sweet man. When my father was about three, he scratched the dining table when visiting his grandparents. He knew he had done a horrid thing and was frightened. His grandfather put his finger to his lips and rubbed a walnut into the scratch to make it disappear. None of the women in the house had to know.

*Q: (laughs)*

DAMMARELL: I don't know if he ever saw any of his siblings after he left Prince Edward Island. There are no family records, no papers or letters or pictures. He had the one boy, my grandfather, whom I remember only from his funeral. He died when I was about three. I had been told he was in heaven. So I went to Gilligan's Funeral Parlor with my grandmother and saw my grandfather stretched out. He had rosary beads and a missal in his hands. That confused me, because I knew you could not read and say the rosary at the same time. I was disappointed that heaven was so ordinary and asked my grandmother, who was kneeling in front of the coffin, if this were heaven. She turned and said, *"Shh!"* It was the only time she ever reprimanded me. That's all I remember of the man. His name was Luke. He married my grandmother, Nora Hannon, who was born in Tipperary. She came over to this country to escort her younger brother, Will, who was too young to travel alone. He had a job with somebody in Kentucky where they raise horses. I don't know if he trained horses or if he rode horses.

My grandmother was born in 1865. So it was a generation right after the famine and Ireland was very poor. I find it interesting that they had the money to let Nora come with him. Grandmother did go back to Ireland after about a year. She was a young woman in her late teens. By that time her brother Michael had married and had brought yet another woman in their house. Nora decided to return to the States. She went to Cincinnati because her first cousins, Mary and Anne Moore, had left Ireland and were working there for either the Proctors or Gambles. I don't know which family.

There was a network of middle class, upper class businesspeople, Protestant Irish who hired Irish maids and cooks. A large segment of Cincinnati was Irish. The Moores got grandmother a job with the Gano family taking care of their little girl. She lived with the Ganos until the child went east to college. Grandmother herself only had four years of education. She had scarlet fever and was taken out of school, but she was one of the best-spoken women I've ever come across. She had total control of the English language. She read and she loved poetry

*Q: Oh Yes, I had a grandmother of Irish ancestry who read to me. I have wonderful memories of that.*

DAMMARELL: As you know, the parish church was the center for social events at that time. The Irish would get together to play music and recite poetry. My grandmother used to recite poetry. She was very tall, a good-looking woman. One of the people in that group was a young man, Luke Dammarell. And I say young man because she was in her late thirties and he was 20. What they had in common was Catholicism. Grandmother told me when I was a 10-year-old kid that their first date was a church picnic. They took the trolley car up to the park and she put the picnic basket between them because she didn't want people to know that they were together. So she must have been conscious of their age difference. Luke pursued her and proposed marriage. She was hesitant, but when it was time to go to the parish priest, Mary Moore pushed her out the door saying, "Nora, you're going to go. There are too many old maids in this house." They were married nearly 40 years and she outlived him by twenty years. My father was the only child of that marriage.

*Q: On your mother's side?*

DAMMARELL: Similar story. Irish-English combination. Her mother was born here, but her grandparents were from Ireland. They arrived in New York in the mid-1850s. They lived in New Jersey before moving to Cincinnati. Her grandfather sold shoes. Their only daughter -- my grandmother -- didn't work. She stayed with her parents after high school. She didn't marry until she was in her late thirties. She married a man by the name of Philip Robinson, who was half English and half Irish. They lived in Hamilton, Ohio, which is now a suburb of Cincinnati. Then it was a little community of its own. Philip Robinson had to leave school at thirteen to support his family when his father died. He worked his way up and eventually owned the store where he worked. This early department store specialized in women's clothing and millinery. He made money. He had two children, my mother and her sister. And when my mother was seven, her sister died.

She had contracted rheumatic fever, damaged her heart. Mother lived at home until she was sent to Sacred Heart Academy in Cincinnati for high school. Then a great personal tragedy happened. When she was fifteen her father committed suicide. Unfortunately, the nuns at school just said he was sick. She only found out what had happened by reading the newspaper when she got home. That really had a big impact on her all of her life. I often wonder if he was an undiagnosed diabetic, since that disease runs in the family. He had gone to the Kellogg Health Center in Battle Creek, Michigan shortly before his death. It didn't help.

*Q: And it was a Catholic family too.*

DAMMARELL: It was a Catholic family. Suicide was then considered a mortal sin and suicides could not be buried in holy ground, but he was buried in a Catholic cemetery. I don't know how they got around that.

*Q: Oh, they could say he was temporarily deranged or something.*

DAMMARELL: Yes.

*Q: The priest makes the decision.*

DAMMARELL: Yes. Even when I was a kid, suicide had a social stigma to it. You couldn't say you had cancer either.

*Q: Oh, absolutely. Did your family have either high school or less?*

DAMMARELL: Both my parents had college degrees.

*Q: They did?*

DAMMARELL: They were only children, which probably meant there was more money to spend on their education. Mother went to the

Academy of Sacred Heart for high school and the College of Sacred
Heart. My father went to the public and parochial grade schools in
Clifton and then to the Jesuits: St. Xavier high school and St. Xavier
College. He graduated from law school at the University of Cincinnati.

*Q: And his main business was?*

DAMMARELL: My father was a lawyer. He really wanted to be a
writer or an actor. He realized that wasn't going to fly when his mother
said, "Well, William, you *know* your father has borrowed money for you
to go to law school." So he did, and he was good. I was lucky enough
to see him when he was trying a case in Cincinnati. I'm glad -- wish
I'd done it more often.

*Q: How big was your family? Did you have siblings?*

DAMMARELL: Both my parents wanted to have children, especially
my mother, who didn't like being an only child. They had five children.

*Q: Cincinnati Catholic.*

DAMMARELL: Catholic, that's right, definitely. I lived in a Catholic
environment, a little cocoon. Most of our neighbors were Protestant,
but I went to Catholic school all my life. I socialized with Catholics. My
father had a Jewish law partner, so I knew some Jews. The only blacks
I met were people who worked for us after World War II.

*Q: On the religious side, on your part, how important was Catholicism in
your life?*

DAMMARELL: Oh, it formed me. Common good and service to
others are basic Catholic principles and a natural fit for AID. Every
gathering or celebration -- my parents liked to celebrate, they both were
optimistic people -- was related to a high holiday: Christmas, Easter, St.
Patrick's Day, even St. Valentine's Day. I didn't question my religion. I
just grew up that way. We had to fast before communion, had to go to
mass, to wear a hat or a veil to church.

*Q: Gloves? Yes, my wife went through that.*

DAMMARELL: Definitely white gloves. In fact, wearing a hat and gloves was a social imperative until I was out of college. My first job was with P&G (Proctor and Gamble) and I had to wear both hats and gloves. When I went to Europe for the first time, I noticed *no one* at the airport had them. So I went into the ladies room and took off my hat and threw it away. Liberated. That was in the early sixties.

# EDUCATION OF A
# GOOD CATHOLIC GIRL

DAMMARELL: I grew up, went to school, in the forties and the fifties. We all went to Sacred Heart. It was a small school. There were pluses and negatives. The negative for me was that I had older sisters who were academic stars and I wasn't.

Q: Yes.

DAMMARELL: Do you have siblings?

Q: I hated the girls who could spell better than I could.

DAMMARELL: (laughs) Yes.

Q: And that was every girl.

DAMMARELL: (laughs)

Q: I assume that you were taught mainly in the early years by nuns.

DAMMARELL: Yes, always! Sacred Heart was originally a French order that focused on the education of young women. The teachers were all nuns. The Religious of the Sacred Heart were all college graduates, unlike some teaching nuns of the period. The only layperson at that time was Mrs. Shields, who taught kindergarten.

*Q: There are all sorts of mostly horror stories, but obviously other stories, about nuns.*

DAMMARELL: That might be the experience of others, but I never experienced any horrors. Though as a product of Catholic education of that period, I learned very early on to sit up straight, not to wriggle, not to talk in ranks. If you did you were admonished. I remember going to confession and confessing that I talked in ranks. It's a wonder the priest didn't break out laughing. We went to confession. It seems like an extreme, but I think we went every week. I mean what sins does a seven-year-old have to tell?

*Q: Oh, wickedness just oozed out of all you seven-year-olds.*

DAMMARELL: The nuns were semi-cloistered. That meant they lived within their community and they didn't go out. They had habits -- of course all nuns wore habits at that time. Most of them were well-educated women. When I was a little girl the school didn't have a cafeteria. The students would go the refectory for lunch. It was a hot meal and good too. Some were nice to me because they knew my mother. My mother had gone there. Some were not. It's not that they hurt me in any way. They were just kind of cold. They weren't allowed to strike a child. They were strict. They taught self-discipline so you learned to monitor yourself. During study hall -- when you would do your homework – and when taking essay tests, the nuns would deliberately leave us on "our honor" with the admonishment not to cheat. It did teach me that whether or not the teacher was there, I shouldn't cheat. I came away with that message. I did not question authority, that is until much later in life. That's my only regret.

*Q: Did the priest tell you what movies you could see or what you couldn't see? What books to read, what not to read?*

DAMMARELL: Yes, but it wasn't the parish priest. It was the schools. I knew there were certain books we were not to read and they probably had something to do with sex. Movies were rated. The Legion of Decency also condemned certain movies as morally objectionable.

*Q: Forever Amber I think was. That was one of the books I recall. I'm not Catholic, but I remember. I used to keep an eye on what the index was listing.*

DAMMARELL: So you could read them.

*Q: So I could read them (laughs).*

DAMMARELL: *(laughs)* I don't know how old I was when I wanted to read Gone with the Wind and one of the nuns had put it on the restricted list. I don't know why. I threw a *fit*. I was old enough to know that that was not right, because there was nothing in it. We were given lists of books to read during the summer, like Ivanhoe and Thomas Costain's books. Do you remember?

*Q: Oh yes. A Canadian wrote them.*

DAMMARELL: They were about English history, and that started me off on my love of English history. I was more interested in English history than I was in American history.

*Q: Well, this brings up a question. Earlier on, were you much of a reader?*

DAMMARELL: Yes. Well, I had trouble reading. I probably was dyslexic. They didn't use that word when I was growing up, but I remember I would be passed on to the next grade on the condition that I would read during the summer with my sister Mary. She said, "Well, pick any book." So I got the littlest, thinnest one I could find. It was The Ballad of the White Horse. Do you know that one? Chesterton. It's a story of Alfred of England. So I began. I just didn't understand a word of it. Mary would say, "Well, what does it mean?" I couldn't answer, because I didn't know. I was struggling just to pronounce the words. She got another book -- I think it was called The Mystery of the Half-Cat." I learned to read with her. And it was *laborious*. So I was a slow reader, *but* we had to read in school, there was no question. I also knew it was a value of my parents to read, so that gave me a personal desire. Once I found books that I liked, I took up reading. I still read to this day. It gives me great pleasure.

*Q: Were you a loner or were you one of the gang?*

DAMMARELL: As I said, there were five of us. There were four girls and a boy. And we were all about a year and a half, two years apart. So we formed kind of a little nucleus. I mean if we ever wanted to do something we always had an older sister, a younger sister. My brother was about four years older than I and seemed to be in a different world. He had his friends. The boys in the neighborhood played together. I thought most of the people in my neighborhood were ancient. They were probably six or ten years older than I. I did have friends like Susie Schmidter, who lived about half a mile away. We lived in the suburbs. We would do things together. There was no television, of course. Radio was big. I remember listening to "Let's Pretend" on Saturdays. We played a lot outside with a ball, handball. We walked a lot. We played in the hill behind our house, several acres of undeveloped land with lots of trees. My sisters and I wrote stories. One sister liked baseball. The Cincinnati Reds were going strong and I remember getting in a streetcar and going with her to a game. We were young. The fact that we did that on our own surprises me now and that we had the money to go meant tickets were not expensive.

*Q: I have grandkids. I watch my children and they're caught up in this. They have to ferry them everywhere by car. You know, suburbia and all. And so you get much more caught up. In my time as a kid, and others, we were sort of "OK, be back by 6:30, we're having dinner then."*

DAMMARELL: Yes. That's what it was with me too. We had bicycles and we would go biking.

*Q: You just really cover an awful lot of ground.*

DAMMARELL: I also remember sitting against an old oak tree, reading, and reading. The day would *never* end. You would hear the cicadas, and the heat – Cincinnati weather is like D.C. weather. Those leisurely days are far-gone.

*Q: Yes, I know. What about movies? Were you much of a movie buff?*

DAMMARELL: Yes. I did like movies. Clifton had a movie theater. That was one of the things Susie Schmidter and I would do on Saturdays. We walked, something like a forty-minute walk. They weren't particularly interesting movies. Cowboys and Indians. We loved it when there was a double feature. I think it was a dime. I do remember my father not letting me go to a movie my older siblings were going to. I threw a hissy fit. The movie was "Snake Pit."

*Q: Oh yes, with Olivia de Havilland.*

DAMMARELL: I was too young to have seen that, so he was right. But at the time…

*Q: One that you wouldn't have understood.*

DAMMARELL: I would have been frightened, I think.

*Q: Yes, because it had to do with insanity.*

DAMMARELL: That's the only restriction as far as movies go. Sacred Heart would occasionally have movies. I remember the nuns saying they didn't think I should see "Henry V". My mother must have been there, because she said, "It's all right, she can see it." Now, why you wouldn't want a little kid to see that?

*Q: Charlton Heston or?*

DAMMARELL: No, no. "Henry V" with…

*Q: Oh yes, "Henry V," good heavens, Laurence Olivier.*

DAMMARELL: Laurence Olivier, that's right. Other movies -- we loved Judy Garland and those musicals of the fifties. I remember going downtown by trolley car, the streetcar. Alice and I went down to see "The House of Wax." Do you remember "The House of Wax"?

*Q: Yes.*

DAMMARELL: With the 3D *(laughs)*?

*Q: Yes, the 3D and Vincent Price. You put on cardboard glasses -- with two different colored coatings on each eye and the wax came pouring out all over.*

DAMMARELL: I was disappointed because I wanted it to be different, but it was just kind of wobbly.

*Q: What about winter sports? What'd you do during the winter there?*

DAMMARELL: Well, we were not a particularly athletic family; I'll tell you right now. As kids we played in the snow. We made snowmen. We made angels. If we got wet it didn't seem to matter. We had sleds and a toboggan. We had a hill in the front of the house and Mount Storm Park was near. My classmates played tennis and field hockey, but I didn't.

*Q: One of the big differences happened during the seventies, eighties, and up to the present and will continue, I'm sure. Young women got much more involved in athletics. Earlier the schools didn't encourage this particularly. You know, a little running around on the playground, but not much.*

DAMMARELL: Recess.

*Q: But now it's the same program for girls as for guys.*

DAMMARELL: And that's a good thing. We had calisthenics. In high school I played basketball and volleyball at Ursuline.

*Q: Yes, volleyball. Yes, there's been a real change and quite recently. Did little Catholic girls play doctor with the boys or not, or?*

DAMMARELL: What boys?

*Q: Oh, there weren't --*

DAMMARELL: Oh, are you kidding? And when I was a girl, there were boy schools and girl schools. Public schools and parochial schools were coed. We were always sent to private schools.

*Q: Well, did they have the equivalent after-school cotillions?*

DAMMARELL: Yes.

*Q: Dancing.*

DAMMARELL: *(laughs)* We had proms. When I was a little girl my older sister would go to tea dances. I associate that with World War II. Most of the boys came from Xavier. I went to Catholic schools in Cincinnati through college. The Mercy nuns started a college for women in the early thirties after Sacred Heart College closed. They had nuns and lay-teachers. Up until that time I had mostly nuns. That was the norm. As you see, I grew up with a lot of women in habits. I was very accustomed to the society of women.

*Q: Was Proctor and Gamble a real presence?*

DAMMARELL: Oh God, yes. It still is. It's a physically big building right downtown. Everybody buys P&G products.

*Q: You went where to college?*

DAMMARELL: I went to Our Lady of Cincinnati College and graduated in 1960. It was an all girl school then, but is now part of Xavier University.

*Q: Did you major in anything there?*

DAMMARELL: I did. I majored in English literature and minored in history, European history. Of course going through a Catholic college you automatically had a minor in philosophy, Thomistic philosophy. You didn't even have an option not to get it.

*Q: Did you ever find yourself sort of challenging either internally or otherwise Catholic doctrine?*

DAMMARELL: No, I did not. I didn't have a questioning mind in matters of religion. I did have trouble with some of the doctrines, but I didn't question them, even if they didn't make sense to me. I began to question during the 1960s after Vatican II, that great wonderful period of social upheaval. Vatican II was heady, very heady stuff. It was wonderful. I continued my interest in theology and when I left USAID (United States Agency for International Development) I went to the Washington Theological Union to study theology. Earlier, after working at Proctor and Gamble, I had lived in Europe for a couple of years, which was very broadening.

*Q: When did you become aware of the American world as opposed to the European -- in other words, events in the United States?*

DAMMARELL: My father was in politics. So I was aware of the political system just because of living with him. He was a Common Pleas judge. The governor had appointed him to complete the term of a judge who died. Judges are elected officials in Ohio. Father was a Democrat in a Republican city. He ran in 1950 and lost. During that period we all worked on the campaign, stuffed envelopes, and saw him give a lot of speeches. I didn't like having to go to the public events. It was hot and sticky and people would stare at you. I didn't like the politicking but learned the routine. Because my parents were Democrats I had warm feelings towards President Truman. When he came through town my mother took us down to the railroad station so we could wave as the car went by.

My parents had European friends. I remember German visitors sitting on the back porch during the summer and talking about how difficult it was locating members of their family after the war. I became aware of Hungary, China, and India because my parents had friends from those countries. A Chinese priest taught us how to use chopsticks. So, yes, I did have the sense of non-Cincinnati.

I was a child during World War II and remember being frightened by an air alert. We had to get to a secure place – we got under the dining room table – and planes flew overhead and dropped leaflets. My grandmother Robinson brought out a box of Mullane candy. I remember eating candy, listening to the noise, and picking up the paper afterwards. That was our invasion. We had a victory garden, wild onions and tomatoes. Then the war ended. It was on a Sunday, we had just come out of mass and as we walked into the street – this was Downtown Cincinnati – *everyone* rushed into the street. It was instantaneous. Every one was very happy because the war was over. Father booked us into the Sinton Hotel, which was right in the center of town. The room had a balcony so we could sit on the balcony and watch the people on Fountain Square. Friends would come up. It was thrilling. We spent the night there. That was the end of World War II and the rationing.

*Q: Well, when the Cold War was going strong were you at all thinking about that, or not?*

DAMMARELL: Well, I knew that Eisenhower was well loved by Cincinnati. The Cold War period was the fifties. I must have been brain dead. I mean as far as I was concerned -- I was not afraid -- wait a minute. Yes, I was. We always were praying for the conversion of Russia. I remember hearing about China, and I was afraid -- see my Catholic training -- I was afraid that somebody was going to come up and say, "Are you a Catholic?" And if I said yes, somebody would poke chopsticks in my ears.

*Q: I'm ten years older than you. But I remember there was a significant divide between Catholics and non-Catholics.*

DAMMARELL: Oh, there was.

*Q: I mean this was done on both sides. I mean at least the religious leaders were more or less saying don't mix, don't mingle, you don't want to marry…*

DAMMARELL: Right.

*Q: I mean, I was told if you marry a Catholic girl your children will be raised as Catholics. I was sixteen years old. I remember that.*

DAMMARELL: I do too. Catholics were to marry Catholics. If you didn't, the marriage was called a *mixed* marriage. You were not married at the main altar. You were married at a side altar. And yes, your spouse had to agree that the children would be raised Catholic. The first time I went into a Protestant church I was in the seventh grade, walking down the street with friends. The door was open to the church and I thought, "Well, I'm going to see what it's like inside." I ran in. It was quiet. And I thought, "Why is this forbidden territory?" But I felt like I had done something very bold. The first time I went to a Seder I was working for Proctor and Gamble and in New York for a few days. A friend invited me to a Seder, which was the first Jewish ceremony I attended. I was full-grown before I attended any Protestant services.

There was a big divide. It was very simple. There was a pool of people you met and were expected to marry. In my era I was expected to marry a Catholic and raise children. You didn't think in terms of a career or working. I did know people who worked. They were considered intellectuals, professors, or their husbands had died in the war and the women had to get a job. It was a different time. The Jewish boys that I met at a soda shop in Clifton, Steir's drugstore, were buddies. We used to sit and laugh and have fun, but there was never a question of dating. I didn't know any black boys. There might have been an occasional Filipino, but certainly there weren't any Latinos or any other cultures. It was the Irish and Germans.

*Q: How about Italian-Polish?*

DAMMARELL: No. There were some Italians. Annie Castellini was a good friend of mine. Ah-ha, there was another group and that did play a part in my decision making twenty years later. My father was a friend of George Joseph. He was Lebanese and had the Oldsmobile dealership. They were Christian.

*Q: In Ohio there'd been quite an exodus from the south of blacks for jobs. Were you aware of a black community in Cincinnati?*

DAMMARELL: Yes, I was. During the war my parents volunteered as teachers in the archdiocesan high school for blacks. A couple of their students occasionally worked for us. They both went to war. One was killed and the other came back. My initial contact with blacks was with people who worked for my parents. The cook, Bessie True, was especially kind to me. She was a big, loving woman. I suspect that she just gave me a lot of attention since my mother was sick. My mother took me to visit her when I made my first communion. I went into her house. I saw lots of people in uniform. So she must have had children or relatives who were in the military. That's all I remember. There were no blacks in grade school or high school and only one black girl in college. How she managed, I don't know. It must have been tough. She was a year ahead of me, so I didn't know her really well, but she majored in English too. So we would see each other occasionally.

*Q: Did the election of 1960 with Kennedy/Nixon have much of an effect on you?*

DAMMARELL: Oh yes, it was a big deal. I, of course, was pro-Kennedy. We were excited. That whole era we were just talking about, the fifties and the Cold War when people in Cincinnati had bomb shelters and bought extra food and supplies, was threatened and constrained. As I have said, I grew up in a very proscribed environment. Then there was Kennedy. He offered the first sense of excitement and openness. He just charmed me. He charmed a lot of people. I was thrilled when he won. I would say most of my friends in Cincinnati thought it was the end of the world and were very upset about the election. I remember my sister Alice went down to hear him talk and shook his hand. We thought it exciting. Shortly afterwards, I was with Alice when she got married in Europe and stayed a couple of years. I was in Spain when I heard that President Kennedy was killed. It was devastating. I couldn't sleep. We had to wait hours to get bits of information.

*Q: In college, what particularly attracted you to English literature?*

DAMMARELL: Well, I liked reading. I think I consciously selected English Lit because of the professors. There were two that I especially liked, Sally Sue Thompson and Sigmund Betz. They gave excellent lectures. So I think that's really what drew me into it.

*Q: Did you follow much of the history of Asia?*

DAMMARELL: Knew very little about Asia. Yes, my concept of Asia probably would have been Japan because of the war when I was a little girl.

*Q: Korean War? Did the Korean War have any impact on you?*

DAMMARELL: My brother was in the Marine Corps during the Korean War. I was in high school. We knew about the Korean War. I knew about Korea because of the Korean War, but my knowledge of Korea was -- was it 37th parallel—was limited.

*Q: 38th parallel.*

DAMMARELL: I remember my brother talking about the paddy fields, but he wouldn't talk about the war.

# FROM P&G TO EUROPE

*Q: Well, then you graduated and went to work for Proctor and Gamble.*

DAMMARELL: That's right; I went to work for Proctor and Gamble. I traveled all over the country. The reason I worked for P&G when I got out of college was my sister Mary. She was then working for Proctor & Gamble in the legal department. She was not a lawyer but worked in that department. Now, that's a difference. Today my sister would have gone to law school without any question. At that time there wasn't any expectation that she could study law. She came to me and said, "I just heard about a wonderful job in market research. You interview women throughout the country to get their opinion of P&G products."

I liked the idea. I was interviewed and hired. During the training program another young woman told me she was Jewish and said, "Well, you know, you and I were just picked up because they needed a quota for Catholics and Jews." I tend to take people at their word. She might have been making a joke, *or* that might have been the case. I can tell you there were no blacks, so there was probably a restriction on whom they hired. But anyway, I loved the travel and had a lot of fun.

*Q: What were you doing?*

DAMMARELL: Market Research. Proctor and Gamble hired young women just out of college to interview housewives about P&G products. A few young men training to be brand managers also did field research.

*Q: Yes. It still is considered one of the best sorts of training programs.*

DAMMARELL: Yes, I'm sure. I wasn't there for a career. I did it because I liked to travel. P&G did do several things for me that I appreciate. Number one, they taught me about the importance of being on time. You would get a telegram, "Dammarell, meet Kennedy, Hotel Metropole, Boise, Idaho." You would then buy your ticket to Boise. We worked in small teams. The projects lasted about two weeks. We sampled mainly middle and lower middle class. They had A, B, C, D categories. A for the wealthy and D for the poor.

After you got your street assignment you would just begin knocking on the doors. Nine out of ten times women were very eager to talk about Proctor and Gamble products. They were probably bored out of their skulls. I never came across a hostile or threatening person. If they were busy they'd say, "No, I don't want to talk." You would write up the report, and telephone it in. The home office would then send you the written report. When my sister got married in Europe I quit and went to be with her. She was teaching in the American military school in Nancy, France. After the wedding I left to visit friends in Paris. I fell in love with Paris and stayed a year as an au pair. It was *perfect* for me.

*Q: You did that for how long?*

DAMMARELL: I did it for a year.

*Q: What sort of families were you working for?*

DAMMARELL: It was one family. The wife was a friend, a Mexican girl who boarded at Sacred Heart and who used to stay with us during the holidays. They had a fabulous place in the 16th arrondissement. Geraldine Benveniste did not work. Her husband was in business, but I don't know what type. I'm actually still in contact with them. The little girl is now a doctor and is up in Canada. There were three kids. I was free in the morning and attended the Sorbonne's Cours de Civilisation Francaise. In the afternoon about four I picked up the children from school, supervised their studies, fed them, and put them to bed. I was free in the evenings and so I saw a *lot* of Paris. And I walked all over the city, and you know, being a history buff that's the perfect city.

*Q: Oh God, yes.*

DAMMARELL: Every street corner had a plaque. I loved it. The family went to Torredembarra in Spain and I went with them. I stayed in Spain when they returned to Paris. Concha Paddack, a friend of my mother's, was in charge of Georgetown University's junior year in Barcelona. God bless that woman. She invited me to stay with her. I taught English at the USIA Binational Center. Georgetown had a young professor, George Bozzini, who was teaching linguistics at the University of Barcelona to Spanish teachers of English. So I sat in on his classes and learned a bit of linguistic theory. We're still close friends. I had a wonderful time in Spain, and then came back to the States.

*Q: You were in Spain when?*

DAMMARELL: '63/'64.

*Q: So Franco was in power.*

DAMMARELL: Yes, he was. It was very stable *(laughs)*.

*Q: Did you pick up any impressions of Franco's rule?*

DAMMARELL: Yes. The Spaniards I socialized with were mainly artists. There were about six or seven of us. They did everything as a group. One of the girls had a chaperone, an older woman. Other friends would join the group occasionally and I noticed that whenever a particular guy came, the others acted a little differently. When I asked why I was told, "Oh, he will report what you say." This was first time I had encountered such a thing. Most of my friends were apolitical, as far as I could tell. They didn't talk politics, but we were in Cataluña. My friends wouldn't have been pro-Franco at all. They resented the fact that they weren't supposed to speak Catalan, but of course they did. That one incident was the only thing that struck me at the time as political, even though I now know that Franco kept tight control and you couldn't discuss politics freely.

I saw a social class, a division within society, that I didn't see in France. The peasant women -- or the women from the country -- all still wore black. If I saw somebody, young or old dressed in black, I knew right away that she was from the country and that she really wouldn't be socializing with people outside that class. That struck me. People were friendly, outgoing. I also taught some older women -- once again through an Academy of Sacred Heart contact. They were older women who were well heeled and who just wanted to keep up their English. They were probably in their fifties. I met with them once or twice a week as a group and had a conversation with them. That was a very enriching experience too.

*Q: Well, did this give you a taste for foreign work?*

DAMMARELL: It did. I liked it. In fact I was thinking of going to Eastern Europe with an American family to look after their kids. Then I got a letter from my older sister, Mary. It was a long letter. It was *really* a demand that I come back and do something with my life. She thought I was frivolous. I went back; oddly enough she still swayed my thinking. Of course after two years in Europe, especially at this stage of life, it was very difficult for me to go back to Cincinnati. Practically everyone I knew was married and having children.

*Q: You must have been feeling an awful lot of pressure to get married and all that, or not?*

DAMMARELL: Actually, I didn't. I knew society said I should, but it was never discussed in my family. It was not an imperative. I don't remember ever being told I had to do anything. I missed the social life I had in Spain. I came back and there was nobody that I could go out with and life seemed bland.

*Q: Most people get married and that sort of takes them out of circulation.*

DAMMARELL: It does. And I understand that. Especially if you're having kids. That becomes your universe. I remember crying one day because I felt just so miserable. My mother came in and asked what was wrong, and I told her. She said, "Well, why are you here? You have a sister in New York. Why don't you go to New York?" My sister was an actor and married to an actor. I was in New York with her a few months and then I moved to Washington D.C. where I had friends.

*Q: What sort of acting was your sister doing?*

DAMMARELL: Well, in Cincinnati she was with the Shakespearean Theater. In New York she ended up doing -- because she got married and had kids -- commercials and some TV work. Her husband was a working actor. You would never have heard of them. He did Off Broadway, Saturday Night Live, soaps and commercials. Joseph Papp had hired her to do something; I forget what the play was. But she found out she was pregnant, so that put the end to that.

*Q: Papp was renowned for putting on things in Central Park and all, wasn't he?*

DAMMARELL: Uh-huh. I don't know what the production was. They had a theater in Central Park. They also had Shakespeare in the Park here in D.C. They still do, don't they?

*Q: I think they still do something like that.*

DAMMARELL: I remember my sister and her husband came to DC as actors one summer when I was living here.

*Q: Well, OK, so eventually after a bit in New York...*

DAMMARELL: Then I came to D.C.

# USAID: OFFICE OF INTERNATIONAL TRAINING

*Q: This is the mid-sixties?*

DAMMARELL: This was 1965, January 1965. I had to find a job. Concha Paddack invited me to a dinner party one night and sat me next to Isabel Galloway. Isabel worked for AID. At the end of the dinner she said, "Why don't you come down to my office, because I know they're looking for an administrative assistant at the Office of International Training?" That's how I got a job with AID. I was not real clear as to how AID differed from State Department. The whole thing was kind of a blur.

*Q: Yes, I think for anybody. I've always in my own mind sort of felt it's all one and the same anyway. I know if you get into the administrative side of things it gets quite complicated, but...*

DAMMARELL: It was a great job for a young woman.

*Q: What was your job?*

DAMMARELL: My first job was with the Office of International Training. I gave the administrative orientation to new participants. We called the people that AID sponsored "participants." They could have been in the States on long-term training, as undergraduates or postgraduate, or on specialized training. They also could have been on a short on-the-job training program.

*Q: Well, who are we talking about? These are people we sent from abroad to come here?*

DAMMARELL: Yes, they were. The missions would have selected them as part of an AID project, to come over here to study or to be exposed to the American way.

*Q: Was there a difference between this and the normal State Department exchange program?*

DAMMARELL: Yes, I think the State Department programs were generally for the movers and shakers and for a shorter time period. That's my impression. Our participants tended to be younger. At that time there were many countries that did not yet have colleges, so there were lots of participants in education. I'm thinking of the African countries. Brazil also had a huge program. My first job was to meet and greet, brief them on what to expect the first few days. Some had never left their village before. Some had to learn everything, how to use a revolving door and turn on the TV and how to use the shower and how to go out and order food. I used to take them to cafeterias so they could just point. They could very well have been the leader in their village. They were selected to come because they had demonstrated some leadership quality, I'm sure.

*Q: Did you get involved in some of this training?*

DAMMARELL: No, I did not. We had people in the Office of International Training who arranged the training programs and kept track of the participants. They had contracts with the various universities where the participants studied. If a participant was coming for specialized training, the AID officer had to develop that training program. Sometimes participants were here for six-weeks, specializing in a particular industry. Others came for an academic degree. This was all done in conjunction with the missions.

*Q: You say training, such as a petroleum engineer?*

DAMMARELL: Yes, it could be that. The participants would return home and work in their countries. AID programs at that time were most likely to in the fields of agriculture, education, and health. Many of the returned participants subsequently became the political and professional leaders of their countries.

*Q: Did you get involved in the people coming here and the intricacies of American life? In other words, at a certain point they pass their early training but they've gone to the university and they seem to be having problems.*

DAMMARELL: I didn't do that. There were people at the universities, campus coordinators, that AID paid for to help the participants. Now, if an individual had a particular problem and wanted to contact AID directly, they would call the Office of International Training and talk to the officer who had designed and facilitated their program. And yes, I think a lot of the people had a difficult time, especially if they left behind lots of friends, a strong social network. We Americans tend to be very independent.

*Q: I would think particularly hard for Africans because of that sort of village culture, which now that we look at it we realize how important it is for anyone.*

DAMMARELL: Important, yes.

*Q: Wish we had more of it. But at the time it was considered sort of a detriment in a way.*

DAMMARELL: It was something that had to be "overcome."

*Q: Uh-huh.*

DAMMARELL: AID normally did not participate in the arts. But we did have an artist from Africa. I don't remember which country it was. He had limited English. He kept his money in a brown paper bag. When he got on a bus or paid for his lunch, he just opened the bag up and asked the guy to take the money out. He was *very* sweet. I don't think anything ever happened to him.

*Q: How did you find working in AID at the time?*

DAMMARELL: You mean how did I like working?

*Q: Yes..*

DAMMARELL: I loved it. I was young. It was my first real job, outside of P&G. I thought it was exciting to see all of the different people who came from many countries wearing -- many of them wore their native dress. I became much more aware of the world. When I would look at a map I would say so and so was from here. For the most part the people I worked with were nice and friendly. I met admirable people, people of integrity, who as a rule really cared about the participants and about their training.

After about a year or two I worked with a man called Charles Wisner who had set up the Evaluation and Follow-up office. He kept in contact with the missions about the participants after they returned home. If the participants came through Washington at the end of their training, I would give them an exit interview. It was basically just to find out about their experiences, what they gained, what they liked, if they had any issues. There was nothing CIA (Central Intelligence Agency) or secret about it. It was just a genuine desire to improve the program. I had a Korean who had come over to get a master's. So he was allowed three years and no more. Within that period of time he had gotten a PhD. I was gobsmacked by that. He must have done nothing but study.

*Q: I served three years in Korea as consul general. My favorite story is I had a young file clerk who said her brother had gotten a couple scholarships to schools in the United States, and asked which ones I would recommend he take. I said, "Well, we've got a lot of these places, but what does he want?" Well, he wanted to be an engineer. I said, "What are the schools?" She read from a piece of paper: "One is Massachusetts Institute of Technology and the other is California Institute of Technology." I thought, oh my God. In Asia the emphasis on education is astounding.*

*In these exit interviews did you see any particular things that struck these foreign exchange participants about America being different from other places, or not? Does anything stick in your mind?*

DAMMARELL: To be honest, if they did say that I don't remember, because it's been so many years. Basically they were glad that they had succeeded in their program. Occasionally you'd come up with people who had an issue, who were unhappy about something; but the norm was that they were happy. They felt successful. The University of Michigan conducted a week-long communication seminar for departing participants to discuss their experience in the United States.

The participants were generally upbeat, but I remember one who was not upbeat. I wonder whatever happened to him. He was an Indian Sikh. He had been here for about three years and was going home. He questioned whether he should cut his hair. He did. The ramifications of that when he got home must have been horrible. So maybe that was an example of somebody who was testing his boundaries.

*Q: Yes. One realizes one reason why Sikhs wear turbans is to cover up their hair. keep it in order. I mean, it's part of the religion.*

DAMMARELL: Yes. The Office of International Training also had Christmas programs when schools were closed down. They offered home hospitality in various parts of the country so that the participants could have an opportunity to see another part of the country. The ones in New Mexico were always extraordinarily popular. The office secretaries made arrangements for these extracurricular activities.

In the early '70s, the Office of International Training got a new director, a political appointee. He noticed some of the secretaries were unhappy. He asked me to talk with them to find out what the problem was. I met with those who were disgruntled and the first question I asked was, "What is it that you want?" That is a *very* difficult question to answer. I didn't know I was asking a difficult question, but that was a difficult question and it was difficult later on when I asked it of myself. That was a time of sexism, racism, and women didn't have the same training, education, and opportunities as men. And it was just bubbling up. I had recently taken a course, "You and Your Career" or something like that at George Washington University.

It was a woman's studies program. I looked through my course papers and developed a program based on my notes. I asked personnel to hire somebody to give the women a management course. The secretaries were angry because they worked for people who could get management training but they could not. They thought it was a putdown. Personnel agreed and gave me a man's name. Although I did not identify myself as a feminist at that point -- even though I was, I didn't think of myself as one. I told Personnel, "No, no, we need a woman. These are all women."

Now, I should have said we need a black woman, because most of them were black, but I didn't think of that. They hired somebody who had done assertiveness training on the East Coast. Jenelyn Block was her name. *Hugely* successful, hugely successful. By word of mouth, her course spread from the Office of International Training to the State Department to the World Bank. That woman worked in Washington for a number of years doing these programs. When I look back on it I understand completely how it fit into that time. It was a totally natural progression of where we were socially.

*Q: What was she covering? I mean things that had not been covered before.*

DAMMARELL: Oh, it's so simple. You have to remember, we are dealing with the sixties, 70s. Consciousness raising, the feminist movement, bra burners, outgoing people who could take a political stand, and Bella Abzug. Most people were not there.

*Q: No.*

DAMMARELL: The majority of women were not there.

*Q: But the issue was there.*

DAMMARELL: The issue was there. Our level of consciousness was awakening. Jenelyn taught assertiveness training, how to say yes and how to say no, how to think out what it is that you can and want to do and not be sidetracked. She was very sensitive to office politics, meaning you could offend your boss very easily and hurt yourself in the process without knowing it. Lots of role-playing. It was a very active training session.

*Q: Well, during this time the debate was raging over Vietnam and our involvement there.*

DAMMARELL: Right.

*Q: Two-point question: How did you feel about it and were you getting any reflections of this from the exchange people?*

DAMMARELL: Oh, how did I feel about it? I was caught up in it. I did not want us to be in Vietnam. I wanted to withdraw. There was so much that was going on. I remember being offered a chance work in Vietnam. I was never unhappy in Washington, but I always assumed I would go back overseas. Part of me wanted to go because I'd never been to Asia and I thought that it would be fun. I wasn't afraid. I have an unrealistic approach to life. Things like that don't frighten me. But I thought, no, politically I can't do it because I'm taking the position that we should be withdrawing from Vietnam and I don't want to support our efforts there.

So that's the only stand I took. Even though I opposed the war, I found the protests very troubling. I grew up with a great deal of security. So when I saw the cars overturned in the streets of Washington and cars on fire I was distressed. At the same time, there is that adrenaline that kicks in and there is a degree of excitement. When you're with a group of people, whether it's a protest or you're watching a protest or something's going on around you, you get a high out of that. I did too.

*Q: Well, did you find that the energy, negative and positive, and just the excitement, but also other things, really affected your working environment?*

DAMMARELL: No. I blithely go on working. I have a project and I do it. Even when I was in my other post overseas, that's what I did. The world could be crashing down, but if I have something I'm going to do, I do it. The killing of our leaders, of course Jack Kennedy was dead by that time, but when they killed Martin Luther King and Bobby Kennedy, that was terrible. I never thought not to work, but it was a downer. I thought, "We're killing -- we're shooting our people, just like in uncivilized countries." So that was painful. Then in D.C. people set fire to the city after Martin Luther King was shot.

Maybe I was a little bit afraid during that time. I was in a training session somewhere downtown. Somebody came into the room and said, "We're stopping this and you are not to go back to the office. You're to go directly to your home." We didn't know what it was. We were inside a building; the room probably didn't have windows in it. When I walked out I saw the streets were crowding up with people and cars were honking. It was clear that something was going on. Then of course we learned what had happened. I started to walk home.

I lived downtown at that time. As I crossed the street I heard some young people saying, "I'm going to go home and I'm going to get my gun." And I thought, oh God. I didn't actually know the depth of the seriousness. I knew it was serious and I knew it was local, but then I began to get telephone calls from my family throughout the country. Then there was a curfew. I never experienced one before. The next morning I got up eager, even though we had only one day of curfew, I was chomping at the bit to get outside, to be free. So I went outside early in the morning, let's say 6:00. I walked up to DuPont Circle.

*Q: Where did you live?*

DAMMARELL: 1020 19th Street. So, right downtown.

*Q: Right in the center of town.*

DAMMARELL: It was maybe a ten-minute walk to DuPont Circle. I could smell the remnants of teargas. That was another thing that shocked me, because I never experienced teargas. There weren't many people. There were some people in the park. DuPont Circle, as you know, used to be where people would gather and play drums and smoke pot and do whatever.

*Q: Yes.*

DAMMARELL: They kept up a curfew and then I saw the military, maybe they were the National Guard.

*Q: As I recall it, the thing that really got me was the 101ˢᵗ Airborne, our elite unit, with full combat uniforms walking up Wisconsin Avenue and standing on corners. I mean, it was not real.*

DAMMARELL: I never felt any personal harm, but I knew it was a dangerous situation. Also I knew people could have tempers and something could happen. They had curfews at 4:00 in the afternoon. Do you remember that?

*Q: Yes.*

DAMMARELL: It's broad daylight. I definitely paid attention to those curfews.

*Q: One of the things that struck me as I was part of the exodus going out to Bethesda. Was seeing African Americans, who obviously were working in Georgetown, waiting for a bus to get them back, and the smoke was coming from there. And I was thinking how awful it was because it was the black part of town that was getting burnt.*

DAMMARELL: Yes. 14ᵗʰ Street.

*Q: Yes.*

DAMMARELL: It was gutted. And it was gutted, as you know, for 20 years. It's now being revived.

# AFGHAN DESK

*Q: Did you want to stay in your job at the Office of International Training?*

DAMMARELL: No, I was very happy there, but something came up and I took advantage of it. Roger Carlson was looking for an assistant on the Afghan Desk. I got the job. I moved from the Office of International Training annex over to the State Department building. I must tell you, I liked that because I was enough of a little girl from Cincinnati, Ohio to be impressed. I guess Roger or somebody took me upstairs to those rooms on the seventh floor.

*Q: Yes, the Diplomatic Reception Rooms. Well, you were with the Afghan Desk from when to when?*

DAMMARELL: OK. I -- let me see -- I'll say -- I'm not real clear about it. I'll say '76. Ambassador Dubs was killed in '77?

*Q: '79.*

DAMMARELL: I went over to Afghanistan for an orientation visit shortly after I was on the desk. I was there for about four weeks visiting all the projects. I loved Afghanistan. The people were tall and proud and they hadn't been conquered and you felt that in them. It was an isolated but beautiful country. I saw Bamiyan and am I glad of that -- those huge statues of Buddha that were carved into the wall --

Each region was a little bit different. I did go north to Mazar-i-Sharif, which is right at the border of Russia. And for me, who grew up in fear of Russia, our major adversary, that was pretty awesome. The next year I was to go for my second visit and about a week before I was to leave we got word that Ambassador Dubs had been kidnapped and murdered.

*Q: Yes.*

DAMMARELL: We had to close the mission. Roger left on another assignment. I stayed to close down the AID program -- and it took about a year and a half to close it. It was very painful to hear of all the doctors and the educators who had been killed. And the schools -- because we had just begun to build girl schools. there were not many, but there were girls schools -- were being built next to the boys schools. When girls reached puberty at about nine or ten they had to withdraw from school, because they could not be with boys. Most girls had only three or four years of education. But we were doing an experiment in which girls could go to grade school for more years. We had also developed a grade school curriculum. Those schools were torn down -- anything that had the USAID handshake on it was targeted. And Russians were there for some time. And we all know the history.

*Q: What had you been doing on the Afghan Desk?*

DAMMARELL: What kind of work?

*Q: Yes.*

DAMMARELL: USAID had a desk and the State Department had a desk, and the desks were the liaison between the mission and Washington. If Washington wanted to have a congressional report, which you know we did every year on our projects, we would have to get the material together. But we could only get the material from the mission. So that would be one task. Anybody that would be coming in from or going to Afghanistan contacted the desk officer to set up appointments. You never knew what was going to cross your desk. Anybody interested in Afghanistan or USAID in Afghanistan could call you. And so you could get all sorts of requests. It could be something very simple, like a form or information about the Afghan program.

*Q: As I recall, particularly until all hell broke loose, AID had a very successful program there.*

DAMMARELL: They did.

*Q: I mean, for a while we were working with the Russians. In a way they were doing their thing and we were doing our thing. But our roles were connecting. Would you say that there was considerable emphasis on women and women's issues?*

DAMMARELL: The big projects in Afghanistan when I was on the desk were in the Helmand Valley. Water, agriculture, irrigation were important, and primary health and primary education. It was under Jimmy Carter if I'm not mistaken. As you know, a project takes a number of years to design. So if you were going to develop project X, you would have to gather material, get the experts, the technical people, to go out and to observe what was needed, determine how to implement it. It took two, three years to get it all together and then eventually, when it was ready, it went through the system in Washington to get approved and to get money allotted. AID started to require a Woman in Development study for each major project to determine what impact the project would have on the lives of women. We didn't have that information.

Those write-ups must still exist today. They must be very interesting for researchers. We hired anthropologists mainly to do studies of women in a particular country and to learn of their status to determine how a particular project would hinder or help women. In the beginning these studies were just kind of pooh-poohed by some, when they were mentioned eyes would flutter. Eventually they were accepted, and now I suspect even today they are done. And then there were the environment studies. AID started to look at the impact a project would have on the environment. So they would have to have an environmental study. This was very early, and they were not easily accepted. Some people were uncertain about the need and effectiveness of doing these studies.

*Q: Oh, Yes. I can recall when I was in Korea when Carter came in and human rights came to the fore. It wasn't my concern, because I was working consular affairs, but it was a pain in the ass.*

DAMMARELL: That's right.

*Q: And you know, we had a dictator. But he was rather benign, the father of the present president of South Korea. He was doing good things for his country, but human rights wasn't...*

DAMMARELL: Yes.

*Q: I've heard complaints about the AID bureaucracy being such a drag.*

DAMMARELL: Well, it really is. And I didn't know how much it was until I went overseas. One of the reasons why I loved working overseas is you have much more freedom. Washington was highly structured, and at that time we had long airgrams that had to be cleared. It was never one or two clearances. It could easily be six, eight, ten. And you had to take that document around to each person and if someone made a change it would have to be re-typed and re-cleared.

# TO LEBANON

*Q: After that job, when and where did you go?*

DAMMARELL: AID personnel was looking for somebody to go to Lebanon and asked me. I said yes, because I had known Lebanese as a kid and liked them. That was my *sophisticated* response. I knew there was a civil war but didn't know exactly what that meant. I knew that there was danger of some sort. I wanted to have some basic training in Arabic and I remember saying I should at least know how to say "duck," you know, "get out of the way." AID didn't require Arabic, because most Lebanese spoke English or French. I had about a week or so of training at FSI in area studies. They might have had some emergency preparation. I guess they did, because I knew to be prepared you should have a suitcase with essentials ready in case you had to leave suddenly. I left in August of 1980. When I arrived in Beirut I was not prepared for the World War II images that I saw going from the airport, driving along the Corniche toward the embassy. The embassy was right on the Corniche.

*Q: Corniche means a coastal boulevard.*

DAMMARELL: A coastal road right along the Mediterranean. The water was pretty, but the buildings were bombed out and there were checkpoints. I forgot how many different militias there were, but there could have been nine, ten, twelve, thirteen. Each group had a section of the city to guard. As I got near the embassy -- the area was called Ain El Mraiseh -- I could see that some houses were in relatively good condition. Over near the water was a great big bombed out area that was isolated. You had to go through it along the port to get to the Green Line (the border between East and West Beirut). When you drove along that little strip, that port area, you saw multiple colored boxcars, red and green and yellow. It looked like abstract art. On one of the bombed out buildings, in giant print, was "Crisis Tourism." Somebody had a sense of humor. That section used to be the nightlife area. The drivers talked about the Kit Kat Club. Of course there was no Kit Kat Club left when I was there.

Our living arrangements were quite good. I had a three-bedroom apartment on the Corniche, about a five-minute walk from the embassy. It was very comfortable. We had electricity. We had water. We had washing machines too. We did not suffer. Later on in '82 the electricity went down for a period of time. By that time I was living in East Beirut. The Americans had a comfortable life. The city of Beirut was an open market; it was like a black market. Everything was for sale, always open. You could get delicious fresh fruits and vegetables from the people on the street with their carts. Some entrepreneurial guy set up a cardboard box wine shop on the street open twenty-four hours a day. If you wanted to buy perfume it would be the same deal, you'd just go to another street corner. They had regular shops too. There was a grocery store called Smiths.

*Q: Would you describe the situation? I mean, what was going on?*

DAMMARELL: Well, in the very beginning when I was there -- I would say for the first several months -- it was quiet. We were not allowed to drive a car at that point. We had to use a driver, an AID driver. We often traveled with a Lebanese colleague. I remember saying, "I can't believe that this is really work." I visited the project sites and it was very calm. We worked with the Ministry of Reconstruction. AID had a five million dollar program at that time. We helped fund the reconstruction of schools, old people's homes, and hospitals damaged by the war. We also had contracts with local Lebanese and U.S. NGOs, such as Save the Children and the YMCA (Young Men's Christian Association) to set up projects to give work to young men, because unemployment was so high. The thinking was if we gave them jobs, if they had work, they wouldn't join the militia. We coordinated with

UNICEF (United Nations Children's Fund). There were also some small projects to help people who lost their businesses due to the fighting. I remember working with a guy who had had his beehives destroyed.

*Q: During this early period when you were there, what were the militias up to?*

DAMMARELL: Well, militias are private armies. I don't have a military background, so in the beginning they all looked like military or police. Some didn't wear uniforms. Some did. They each had their own checkpoints. Sometimes they'd be in a little house, but more often than not they would just be standing there. We had diplomatic plates so they knew we were Americans. If they wanted to stop us, they would. But usually they waved us ahead. But it was a bottleneck, because if we were behind a car that didn't have a Dip plate, we'd have to wait for them to go through. Everybody was armed. They all had guns. And of course they had bullets in them! I remember somebody from Washington came and he said, "Well, they all have guns. But do they have bullets in them?" *(laughs)*

A couple of times we were stopped even with our Dip plates. I remember somebody was trying to sell some sort of brochure to get money. But it was more a nuisance than anything else. I knew that during the civil war -- it began in '75 -- there were times when a Muslim or a Christian wanted to retaliate for the killing of one of his own would pull someone out of his car at a checkpoint and shoot him. I knew that it could be very serious, but I felt safe because I was an American. This was naive. I felt safe because I was an American and a woman. At that time they weren't killing women. It was kind of unreal. I was not afraid. One of the first nights I was in Beirut, I heard somebody running down the alleyway and somebody running after him. That did frighten me, because I knew somebody was being chased. Then the next morning I woke up and it was a beautiful day and there was a parade of tanks going down the Corniche just in front of my apartment. Bizarre. But for some reason, I adjusted pretty quickly.

*Q: Let's talk about your job a bit. When you got there what were you doing?*

DAMMARELL: When I got there Peter Cody was the AID rep. There were only two people, Peter Cody and Ernie Pop, prior to my arrival. Ernie was the only general development officer and Peter decided he needed to have two. I was the second general development officer. So there were only three of us. Ernie did the more traditional program officer work, developing the budget and working with the government contacts. I mainly managed contractors like CRS (Catholic Relief Services). I got to know all the AID projects. We made field trips to oversee the progress of the projects, to see how the money was being spent, to see if people were actually working on the projects. So basically I did a lot of traveling around the country, which is very small and beautiful. I liked it a great deal. Baalbek was wonderful. Hezbollah didn't exist during the first couple of years I was in Beirut. During one of our visits to Baalbek in 1982, we noticed a large house with a huge black flag in front of it. The driver avoided that house, telling me, "Oh no, we don't want to deal with them." Well, they turned out to be the nucleus of Hezbollah.

*Q: Well, you know, the term Levantine has a certain ring to it, as to Lebanese being rather sharp traders.*

DAMMARELL: Oh yes.

*Q: How did you find dealing with Lebanese contractors?*

DAMMARELL: I thoroughly enjoyed it. I understood that they were -- wily is maybe a derogatory term. A way of looking at Lebanese behavior is this way. The Lebanese always kept everything open for negotiation because they could see the possibility of this and that changing. They, the government officials that I worked with, were totally courteous to me. Because it was such a small country you got to know everybody; really, eventually you got to know everybody. They were very respectful.

There was no discrimination because I was a woman. If there was, they certainly never displayed it. They were a refined people who were outgoing, very sociable. And they loved to eat well. So often they would have a mezza, to celebrate the opening of a project or some other event. Now, I was also very aware that people always wanted American visas, from the guy on the street selling orange juice to someone working on an AID project. So I understood that they -- I mean it wasn't my personal charm that they were attracted to, it was the access that I might have, which actually I didn't have, since I was not that high up.

*Q: What was social life like?*

DAMMARELL: I had actually a pretty good social life. First of all, there was no curfew when I was there. I think there is now. Eventually it got to be so safe that we were allowed to have a car. So at one point I had a car. You were advised not to go to any mass gatherings or to the theater. I did go to a movie once or twice. The museum and the Baalbek theatre were closed because of the war. My social life consisted of cooking and having people over for dinner because I like to cook. That was normal for me. It was fun having people over and talking. Also, because I'm a Roman Catholic, I would go to mass at the Franciscan church, St. Francis, and I met some people there: the French Canadian ambassador's secretary and a couple of Maryknoll brothers who were studying Arabic on the Green Line, if you can believe it, at St. Joseph's University. I met some Europeans and Americans too. One woman who was married to a Muslim attended mass there. The only time she could get out was to go to mass. It was difficult for me to talk to an American woman who lived such a restricted life. I remember inviting her -- we often would have lunch after mass -- for lunch and she said, "No, no, my husband won't permit it. He won't permit it."

We were allowed to go to Damascus. So I drove over to Damascus I don't know how many times, quite often. One time we drove up to Jordan. We had long weekends, tourism. Once again, I think some of those trips were potentially dangerous, but I was never afraid.

*Q: You've mentioned part of it. What was your observation of the role of women in the country?*

DAMMARELL: I made friends with some Lebanese and they're still friends. Some of them are here in the U.S. now. I met a group of highly educated women of all sects, Christians and Muslims, Shia, Sunni. Women with PhDs, women who ran businesses, who ran schools. Now, my observation was when I was with these women and their male counterparts, the women would be quiet until the men left. They weren't as outspoken when the men were there.

*Q: Well, you must have been by position a senior person in the embassy. And I doubt if there are many other women who were your equivalent.*

DAMMARELL: Well, I was the only USAID woman at one point. I wasn't senior. I was a general development officer. I'm trying to think of other women -- in fact, our USAID secretary was a woman. The secretaries were women. Actually secretaries, especially secretary to the ambassador and DCM, were pretty powerful people. They knew what was going on. Christine Crocker -- Ryan was the political officer -- was working in the political section. Most were men. There might have been CIA women. I made an effort not to know who was with CIA. You knew the station chief because he was identified as the station chief, but I didn't want to know anything that could compromise anybody. So I just didn't ask questions. There were some women there. No, I never felt being a woman was a restriction. At that time there were damn few women who were USAID directors. I think there were only a handful. It's quite different now. It's much healthier now.

*Q: Who was the DCM?*

DAMMARELL: Bob Barrett was DCM. John Gunther Dean was the ambassador when I first got there. And I liked him. He would accompany us on field trips, especially if there were a project ceremony. I'm assuming he did that because he wanted to go talk to local leaders. I remember a big Druze gathering that he came to. I'm sure he really wanted just to talk to Walid Jumblatt. I'd say he came several times, maybe six times a year. Occasionally he'd invite me to drive with him. The ambassador traveled with the lead car, his car, and a chase car. Usually we were behind the chase car in an USAID car with a driver. I remember once going up a mountainside and a car came zooming by and whacked -- hit -- the chase car. All of a sudden everything just stopped and car doors flew open and all these bodyguards with guns were running around like -- it was like the movies. I was startled. I had not seen anything like that before.

Another time when I was driving I saw something -- I don't know what it was -- plop down in front of me and explode. It was far enough ahead that it didn't hurt me in any way. I just turned around and left. I never wanted to visit a dangerous place. So if we realized something was happening we would stop and go back or we'd visit another project someplace else. So that was a reality. I wasn't a brave soul that sought out danger.

A lot did happen, though, when I was there. I can hardly believe it, but I know it's true. As I said, I like to cook and had a big dining room table. When the shells would be lobbed in -- we could tell if they were going out or coming in -- everybody seemed to know and picked up their plate of food and went into the kitchen, because there was a section like a butler's pantry that didn't have any windows. We'd just continue with our conversation until it stopped (laughs). Yes, it was a pathological society. It truly was. It's like these blinds. As I said, I focused on work. I could just pull those blinds down and not acknowledge the seriousness of the situation.

A rocket propelled grenade (RPG) hit AUB (American University of Beirut), which was a surprise. Normally AUB was considered sacrosanct because a lot of people were graduates or had family who went there. An RPG came in and I thought oh, it's just another RPG. I was working in the office on a Saturday. By the way, overseas you could work twenty-four hours, seven days a week. It wasn't that you were supposed to do that, but you got caught up in your projects.

Q: *Oh yes, absolutely.*

DAMMARELL: Then I heard this awful noise and I thought, "Oh, I've got to get away." I ran to get away from the windows. And I made a terrible mistake, because I went back to get my purse. Nothing happened to me, but that was a mistake and it did teach me, from then on I swore I'd never go back for everything. Do you know what a Stalin Organ is?

*Q: It's a multi-shot rocket.*

DAMMARELL: Yes, and it goes *(makes rocket sound)*.

*Q: Yes.*

DAMMARELL: That was the noise I heard. We were not hit. But that was scary.

*Q: Well, what happened? I mean, when you first got there really not much was happening.*

DAMMARELL: I'm trying to think of the timing of this. I just know in the beginning, this was 1980, 1981 -- the big change was '82, but there were other things in '81 -- sometimes Israelis and Palestinians would fire at each other. Israel was in the southern part of Lebanon. The Lebanese didn't have the army in the south, but they had a militia, a Christian Lebanese militia. They would fight periodically. And Syria would get involved. There was always something happening. The big change was when the -- well, I guess it began when the PLO (Palestinian Liberation Organization) were removed. Oh, by the way, Ambassador Dillon had arrived. John Gunther Dean left and Dillon came in. And then I guess Philip Habib was there, negotiating to get the PLO out. He lived in Yarze. When Ambassador Dillon came in -- he lived in Yarze -- he opened up his place to him. That must have been after the invasion. So the first major event was the decision to get Arafat and the PLO fighters to leave. They brought in the U.S. military as part of the Multinational Force to oversee the withdrawal of the PLO.

*Q: Yes.*

DAMMARELL: The PLO left by ship. I was out in the field and the driver said, "Let's go up to see the ships go off." So he drove up to the top of the hill and we stood up there and saw the ships leave. Well, when the PLO left, there was no problem. And then Bashir Gemayel, who was the young leader of the Lebanese Forces, ran and won and was elected president. The people on the Christian side were ecstatic. The atmosphere was almost like the Kennedy feeling. Everybody was happy;

they were in the streets, driving around with large Lebanese flags. And then Bashir got killed. That happened in the afternoon. There was panic. That was on a Tuesday and I remember our driver, Joseph, coming in on Thursday afternoon. He was all excited and said, "They are putting on flak jackets." And I asked, "Who?" and he said, "The Phalange are putting on flak jackets." I didn't understand what that meant. After Joseph left, I went out to Yarze to read the cable traffic.

*Q: Yarze?*

DAMMARELL: Yarze -- that's where the ambassador had his home -- is a suburb in the mountains. Ambassador Dillon was very hospitable. There were people there, mainly State Department people. I associate this time with Philip Habib and Morrie Draper. There seemed to be an increase in staff, in State and the military and also AID. AID was going to become a full mission, increasing to about five or six or seven. This was because peace was going to break out. That's what people said. It was going to be better. The only reason I say that is because Bob Pearson, a USAID intern who spoke Arabic, used to say he didn't see any difference.

When we went to our projects sites we still saw all of the militias, we still saw the people as they were before. But that's an aside. After Bashir was killed, that Thursday night I was in Yarze and I stood outside on the terrace. Underneath there was a swimming pool, I think. We were high up on the hill, so I could look out and see the city. The city was ablaze with yellow flares in the sky. It looked like a nineteenth century stage because of the yellow sulfur-like glow. You could see everything. I had not seen flares like that before. I had heard fighting before, I had seen rockets before, but I had not seen it so constant like that night. I had no idea what it meant. But I remember being very relaxed and having a beer with some guy who had recently arrived. I think he was military.

The next day was Friday. On Saturday morning Bob Pearson and I went to a meeting in West Beirut called by the UN Rep, Iqbal Akhund. He wanted to discuss housing. So when we got there -- by this time we were able to drive -- I think it was 8:00 in the morning -- we found Iqbal and he was confused. He looked really worried. And he said, "I don't know what to make of it, of that woman that just left." We didn't see anybody. "The woman that just left told me a story, I can't believe it." She was Scandinavian, I don't know if she was Danish or Swedish. She was working in a hospital in Sabra-Shatila and reported that people came in and asked if anybody was a Palestinian. When the doctor raised his hand or indicated that he was, they took him out and shot him. She became -- hysterical was the word. She wanted to save the children and was told, "Well, you can only save as many as you can carry out." So she picked up two children and left.

I told Iqbal we'd go back to Yarze -- because the telephones didn't work we had only walkie-talkies -- and report what he'd said and when he got that written report -- because he had asked her to write up a report -- we'd pick that up and bring it back to Yarze. As we left Bob said, "We've got to go to the embassy first to check if they know anything." Well, I should say, we had already moved out of West Beirut and the embassy was closed. We relocated to the east side when it had become too dangerous living in West Beirut. So, we were living on the eastside. When we went to the embassy there was somebody at the door. He said, "No, he had heard nothing." A couple of foreigners, Europeans, came by and Bob talked to them. They had heard similar stories, but they didn't have much information. Sabra-Shatila massacre is what it was. Bob said, "Let's go to Sabra-Shatila." And I said no.

*Q: These were two PLO refugee camps.*

DAMMARELL: Yes, they were. That's exactly what they were. When the Palestinians left Jordan and they settled in -- originally they were welcomed into Lebanon -- the Sabra-Shatila area. They're called camps, but they were suburbs. It was a slum area. It was a poor area. They were mainly Palestinians, but they had other foreign nationals living there too. So when Bob wanted to go there to check it out personally, I said no because I didn't want to -- I said, "I don't want to risk it" and also I wanted to go back and report.

So we drove back and went out to Yarze. Morrie Draper was there and he was *very* upset. He was very worried and pacing about. "What are you doing over there?" Because we were AID we had a little more latitude to travel. We were allowed to visit project sites. We always checked with Ambassador Dillon before going. We weren't -- we didn't go rogue. Draper said, "Go sit down and write your story." He gave us paper and we sat and wrote the story. We thought, "Isn't this weird that they're getting mad at us." We didn't know the magnitude. I asked if Ryan was there and was told he was at Sabra-Shatila. What happened was there were a lot of Palestinians living there, mainly the mothers and wives and children -- and the old men who stayed behind -- of the Palestinian fighters who left with Arafat. These were the people that stayed behind. After Bashir was killed, his militia, the Phalange, invaded -- entered that territory. You know what I forgot?

Q: *The Israelis.*

DAMMARELL: The Israeli invasion. That's what it was! That's why we moved over to the eastside. Let me backtrack. I'll stop now and say -- because this was the key point -- in June of '82 the Israelis moved up from the south. They always were in the south, but they moved up and much to everyone's -- at least *I* was surprised, they moved into Damour, which is very near Beirut. The ambassador called a meeting and said, "All non-essentials will leave tomorrow." And we did. The next day was -- I think it was Sunday; we met at the embassy with our suitcases. The drivers took us on a very circuitous route to get to the airport. We got to the airport and we waited and waited because there was shelling. Finally Bob Pugh called. Bob Pugh was Bob Dillon's DCM. Bob Pugh was with us. He called from the airport, I guess to Yarze. Somebody up there called the States and somebody from the States called the Israelis and said, "Stop the shelling. We've got to get these people out." There was a lull and then the plane took off and we left -- we were the last ones out. We were evacuated.

Kurt Shafer and I were evacuated to Rome. We were there a couple of days and then sent to Egypt. We were there for maybe two weeks. The Cairo mission gave us a little, something like a fifteen million dollar project, which was nothing to them, because Egypt had such a big program. Kurt and I left Cairo and went over to the Sinai. We went around to the various places where the Israelis had set up a post or houses. The real estate that the Egyptians bought was left intact. The places that they didn't buy, didn't pay for, the Israelis tore down. They poured cement in the wells and they salted the earth. Now, that's an expression that meant nothing to me until I saw the salted earth. It's dead. They had grown roses there beforehand. But it was all gray and dead. It was amazing. We would go to the little villages and talk to the people in charge and they would say, "We need X number of dollars to unplug the well or to do X, Y, and Z." We gathered the information and wrote a report and brought it back to the office in Cairo.

It was July when we got word. Bill McIntyre, who was then the AID rep, called Egypt and said that we were to return to Beirut right away because Peter McPherson, who headed USAID, was coming for a visit on July the Fourth. So we went back. We had to fly to Cyprus to get a boat and I remember being in charge of the mailbag. We landed in Jounieh, the eastern part of Lebanon, where the Christians lived. It's a resort area. I'd never been there because we didn't have a project there. I saw people in bikinis and swimming suits. It was all kind of unreal.

From there we moved to the east side. We were not permitted to go back to our apartments on the west side. The west side is Muslim. We moved to Achrafieh, which is the big city in East Beirut. We stayed at the Hotel Alexander for a few days. I was on the roof of that hotel when I saw the shelling of Beirut. It was like a show almost. It was just all night long shelling. No yellow flares, it was just the bright lights of the shelling. And who walks by me but Ariel Sharon. I'm like, "What is this?" You know, he's a big fat man. AID moved out of the Alexander to a little village called Brummana and rented rooms in a hotel for our living and for our office. That's where we operated out of until we got back to West Beirut. We were in Brummana quite some time.

# SABRA-SHATILA

The Israelis occupied Beirut in June. The next time I went to Beirut I saw the Israeli flag flying. I saw -- to me they were young kids -- Israelis in charge and others walking around like tourists. Joe Curtain headed CRS and had to get Israeli permission to visit some project. I was with him at the time and we had to wait and wait and wait. That was new for me, because normally I would just go to a site without seeking permission from anyone.

So that was June, July, August, September. September is when Bashir was killed. Yes, it was September because Sabra-Shatila was in September on the 16th. Bob Pearson and I went to a meeting in West Beirut on that Saturday. Thursday, Friday, Saturday, those people were being killed in Sabra-Shatila. It stopped Saturday morning when word got out. The women, I understand it was the women, took the bodies of the dead because Muslims have to be buried within 24 hours. There were bodies that they couldn't get because the slabs of cement, the sides of the walls of the building, covered them. So once again, Iqbal Akhund called a meeting and the reps -- I don't know who was there, a lot of Europeans -- and asked if anybody would like to go with him to the prime minister to seek permission to have Rafik Hariri's construction workers remove the slabs that covered the dead.

We knew the engineers because of our projects, and Hariri said it would be all right for them to help, so that the dead could be found. I volunteered to go with Iqbal. Surprisingly there was another -- the only other person was a woman. She was Shia from the south. We had worked together. I forget her name. Anyway, the three of us went to see the prime minister to get permission. My French is not that strong, but it was strong enough to know what he was saying. He was *livid.* He kept looking at me and he would do this: he said, "You promised us, you promised us they'd be taken care of, they'd be safe. They'd be safe." Meaning that when the PLO fighters left we promised that we would take care of their families, we would protect the families.

*Q: Yes, the promise had been made.*

DAMMARELL: I felt like I was a worm. It was terrible. Then he gave us permission. We had actually gone to Sabra-Shatila before we went to see the prime minister, gone to Sabra-Shatila to see what to report. When we were there it was isolated. When you walked into that section of town it was like a huge football field, everything was plowed down. It was empty. Then we got to a point where the buildings were still standing. The houses were made of cement. And the façades on the houses that we could see were falling down. They were like dollhouses. You could look inside. And the first thing that caught my eye was a picture of the Last Supper. So I thought, "Oh my God, Christians lived here." I just assumed they would all be Muslims. There was a plate of olives and children's toys. The woman with me said to me, "Look at this -- can we look at this?" It was a huge circle of fresh earth. We found out later that's where a lot of people were dumped, the bodies were dumped. She said, "Can't you see that child's hand?" And I instinctively turned around, didn't look at it.

Then we walked into this maze of houses. You know what these communities are like. You just twist around -- you could easily get lost. There was blood everywhere. By this time it was brown globs and congealed. And it was against the wall. It was everywhere. I didn't step in it, but it was prevalent. There were arrows on the walls. I remember in one section seeing arrows pointing this way to exit, to show you how to get out. There was graffiti. They wouldn't translate for me, so it must have been vulgar. But there was the icon of a little Christmas tree, of the Phalange, that's their symbol. That was there. And they had drawn a penis and testicles next to it. There was something written in Arabic.

We went around to the hospital area -- the blood is the thing that came to me, and the stench. The stench, the sweet smell of death is horrible. We heard a woman wailing, really a wail, kind of a rhythmic wail. There was a woman dressed in black sitting on the ground with her back against a tree wailing. Her husband came out and talked to us. He said, "We've just come back. This is our home. When I had heard them yell -- when I heard them yell I got into my truck and put my children and my wife in the truck and we went out the back way." He worked for the city and had a truck, a city truck. And that's how he got out. It turned out he had two boys. Eventually they came out from inside their home. They were hiding. After about five minutes they came out. They were like fourteen, fifteen. They were kind of stunned, they seemed dumbfounded.

So that was our first exposure. Then after -- I don't know if it was the next day or not -- after we had talked to the prime minister, we went back. This time Peter McPherson must have come a second time, because I think Peter was there. But I'm not sure. Maybe it was just Iqbal. But there was a lot of activity. The ICRC, International Committee of the Red Cross, came in and they had thrown lime over the bodies. So you didn't see bodies. The bodies were desiccated. And Hariri's people were pulling away the debris. It was sad.

The only time other than that that I had ever seen a body was in the south. When Peter McPherson came in July we went down south and there had been some killing. I guess it was the Israelis that had done it, because we were in Sidon. They had not buried their dead. Maybe it was within the twenty-four hour period, and I had seen a woman, didn't know her of course, but she just looked like an ordinary person. Her face was twisted; it was like she was screaming. There was another section where there were a lot of little kids in the corner of a school. I didn't like that. But I was fascinated. I must say, I looked at it and looked at it and looked at it, but I didn't like it.

Sabra-Shatila was different. I didn't see bodies, I just saw white powder.

*Q: This Sabra-Shatila was done by essentially Christian militia.*

DAMMARELL: Yes.

*Q: But there's been many accusations, probably credible, of Israeli, at least if nothing else they didn't stop it.*

DAMMARELL: Israelis were very active in Beirut. First of all, Israel had occupied, they were the occupiers of that city. They stood around. They had guards standing around so that the Phalange militia could go in and not be interrupted. Every Lebanese I ever knew talked politics at a drop of a hat. With Sabra-Shatila, they didn't want to say peep. They didn't want to discuss it. People wept, they cried, but it was a taboo topic. At first we didn't know what had happened. I mean who knew -- at least I didn't know. I wasn't a political analyst, mind you. The first credible account came from an Israeli journalist. Some guy, I thought I'd never forget his name, several days later called for an official inquiry and he laid blame on the Israelis for their role. It was definitely the Phalange who did the killing, but they couldn't have done it alone.

*Q: Sharon, who was the head of the Israeli Military at the time, probably had a hand in this. If nothing else: "Go ahead, be my guest." It was a horrible thing, because these were essentially noncombatants. And they allowed this Christian militia, which was highly motivated by other killings that had happened, to go in and just kill these helpless people. And it's something many people won't forget.*

DAMMARELL: I read some place the official number of dead was one thousand, but the locals would say there were three thousand. It was a big killing, a loss of life.

# THE BOMBING

*Q: Anne, you were in Lebanon from when to when?*

DAMMARELL: 1980 to 1983. I'd been given my onward assignment. I was to go to Sri Lanka, which I really wanted because I knew it was a very small program and I thought there would be nothing going on there *(laughs)*. I was a little bit tired. I loved Beirut, but I was tired. That Monday, it was April the 18th, I stayed home so that I could meet with the contractors who came to look at my stuff to determine what would go by airfreight and sea freight and to get bids. I did that all morning and went in because I had a report to write up. I got to the embassy about 12 noon and ran into Bob Pearson at the front door. He said, "Let's go down to the cafeteria and get something to eat." I said OK, and we went down.

He was going to give me a little farewell party and was going to tell me who was coming and what he was going to do, that kind of thing. We had lunch. Since we were going to just talk business, you know, the party, we didn't attempt to sit up front at the captain's table, where often I would sit to talk to whoever came to lunch. We moved to the back of the room. The room wasn't very big; it was about twice the size of this room. We were chatting away and I saw somebody come in who normally sat back where we were and waved at him. I happened to see Tom Blacka. He had just come. I nodded to him. Tish Butler was there. These were totally inconsequential actions, reactions. But now because of the day they become significant.

All of a sudden I heard a very loud noise. I remember thinking oh, you'll have to tell the children a door slammed, because that's what people would say when a bomb would go off. I leaned over to tell Bob I didn't think it was a bomb. Actually I thought it was a clap of thunder, because the day was overcast. And at the same time that that happened, everything went black and silent and I felt a shock go through my whole body. If you had ever put your finger in a plug when you were a kid, you would know how the electricity zigzags through your finger. That's what happened throughout my whole body. What I thought had happened was I was sitting next to the electrical system for the embassy and that the people who built the hotel, because originally it was a hotel, tried to save money and had put in a flimsy electrical system in the wrong place. One of the wires had fallen out and hit me and I was electrocuted.

Now, I thought further, I'm dead. Maybe that's what I was trying to tell Bob, that I had died. I remember trying to get in touch with Bob and I realized I didn't have a body. I thought -- well, I felt isolation -- it's a feeling, not a thought. It was a feeling of deep -- there was nothing -- I didn't have any body, I didn't have hands, and I couldn't see or hear. So I assumed I was dead. I thought to myself, "This is terrible." It was profound isolation. "I really can't endure this for eternity." Then I started to get mad. I thought, "Well, it's not really fair," my parents had lied to me; all the teachers had lied to me. Then I stopped thinking. So from the outside, what happened looked like a matter of a second or so, but inside your brain you continue to think.

Q: Sure.

DAMMARELL: I was then blown outside. I was unconscious. What happened was this. When the bomb hit, the walls exploded outward, and I went out with one of the walls. Bob Pearson, oddly enough, didn't. He was sitting right next to me. He went up in the air and fell down and never lost consciousness. He said he knew right away it was a bomb. When I woke up I thought -- there was something on my face and I thought it was the wall of the building and I thought I was trapped. I tried -- I said to myself, "Well, just test it to see if you can push that wall away," because I thought it was a concrete wall. I couldn't get my hands to move. I didn't realize both my arms were broken, which is why. This arm, the left arm, was broken so the bones were like that.

But then I began to panic, and I thought -- well, no -- I began to mentally talk to myself like I was another person. I said, "No, relax, just remain calm. People have been in buildings for days, for weeks even; if they can, they'll find you. Somebody will find you." Then I tried again. It's just sheer will. You push. Your mind does control your body in this sense. So eventually I did get my arms up and I saw that it wasn't a concrete wall after all; it broke into little bits, little white chunks, gray chunks. At that time I could move my head. I looked around to see what had happened and I heard, began to hear, moaning. I knew those were the moans of somebody dying.

I looked to my right to see if I could see any bodies or people and I couldn't see anything. I was like in a little shell, real narrow shell. But I did see a flame to the right, which was quite high. It looked like a curtain, a curtain of fire, dramatic orange-red. It was far off. It wasn't near me. I could see that the walls of the embassy had fallen down, but the corners, the bricks, were in place. And that seemed strange. I wasn't in any pain. My jaw ached and that was the only pain I was in.

And then I looked in front of me and I saw that there was this white stuff all over me and that I had blood in my hands. It was real thick, so it was globby. I began to test it, you know, play with it. It was tacky and I began to do this to see how I could pull it off, just to play with it. It was kind of an idle thing to do. Then I looked to my left because I had a *non*-sensation on my left side. What had happened was my ribs had broken and they had severed the nerves. So I didn't have a sensation. But I saw that there was a lot of blood on my left side. So then I thought, "Well, my heart's been punctured and I'll bleed to death." That was my conclusion. I thought, "Well, I'd better see how serious this wound is." And I tried to put my right hand on my left side to see if I could touch my beating heart. And I couldn't get my arm to work properly.

I then looked to my left to see what was going on there. I saw more of this gray matter all over the earth, in the grass. I saw one blade of green grass that stood out. As I looked further to the left I saw a row of flames, not very high, but they were being pushed I guess by the wind. I thought, "Oh, those little flames are going to come and set fire to my hair and then I'm going to die, I'm going to burn to death." And then that's when I really panicked. I really thought I was going to burn to death. I had a great sense of, I guess it's remorse or guilt for not being nicer. You know, I didn't have any great big thought that I wish I had done X, Y, and Z, none of that. It was just that real sense of, oh, this is the end and I could have been nicer.

I saw a curl, a black curl of smoke in the air. The sky was blue, but that black curl of smoke was overhead or floating by and I thought, "Well, if I can inhale that, some of that smoke, then I can suffocate and I won't burn to death." That was how I was thinking. Then for the first time, I called. I thought I'd call Bob and have him help me. So I opened my mouth to shout and nothing came out. Then I tried again. I thought, "Well, if I yell *secours* (help), somebody would come help me. I opened my mouth and I yelled help. Something did come out. It was real soft and I waited a few minutes -- or I don't know, maybe a second or two or thirty seconds until I had the energy again to inhale to get my voice to work again. I yelled again. And then I heard somebody say, "Yalla bina" (Let's go). Four young men came. One was in army fatigues and he had a rifle. They were all just staring at me. They probably saw the other people that were dead there too, because they didn't react to me right away. I remember looking at the military guy and wanting to say to him, "You have to put the rifle down before you can pick me up." But I really couldn't talk.

One of them took the leadership role and began to tell them, the other people, to do something. They tried to pick me up by my shoulders and that was excruciatingly painful. Then I yelled. I heard myself yell. There was something on my left foot. I think it was an air conditioner, but I had no idea what it was. So this guy who was the authority figure, the leader, told them to remove that from my left leg, which they did do. Then they picked me up. They used their arms like boards, because all four of them picked me up. They carried me out.

I remember thinking, "They're going to drop me." I just had that feeling they were going to drop me, "But that is all right, because I've been found and everything is going to be all right." Well, they didn't drop me. They took me up -- by this time they had an ambulance come down. I think a lot of people responded rather quickly. I felt like they swung me in, that the door opened up and they flung me in, plopped me down. There was somebody to the right of me, and I just thought it was a dead body. I have no idea. By this time I couldn't move. I just could look forward, but I couldn't move my neck to the right or to the left. There was a woman, an International Committee of the Red Cross woman, Lebanese, that I knew. I had met her before, but I forget her name.

She was a young woman that I had worked with at some point. And I tried to explain to her that I had a serious heart wound and that I needed blood. But she couldn't understand me and all she would say was, "We're going to be at a hospital soon, just relax, we're going to be at the hospital soon." I noticed how we were driving and it was not the quick route, because the American University of Beirut Hospital is very near the embassy. They were going *all* the way down the Corniche, and I thought, "Why are they taking the long way?" But they got to the hospital.

When they came to the hospital they opened the doors up right away and people came to take me out. Who else was in the ambulance, I don't know. They put me on a gurney. I could see, you know, peripheral vision at this point, I could see a lot of people. There was a lot of activity. One of the doctors who was the head of the medical department and I had seen at some function or other and knew him came up. Or perhaps he was with the Ministry of Health. He knew me and he said, "Now Anne, you're all right, you're all right." Then he left.

I had a sensation that my cart was being pushed down a certain way and I thought, "Well, I'll be checked in." And then I got stopped and I knew that there was some sort of triage, because they were saying, right-left, putting people in different categories. I wasn't in the category that was being tended to and so for a while I thought, "Oh, this must be *really* serious; I'm right, my heart's open and I'm bleeding." But then I didn't die. I was there a long time. A number of people came by. I don't know where I was. It was in the lobby, but I don't know where. I heard somebody that sounded like Bob Pearson, and I thought it was Bob Pearson, talking. And I heard *plink, plink, plink.* So my guess was they were taking shrapnel out and putting it in a little tin basin. Then I thought, "Bob's alive." When I was at the bombing site -- when he didn't respond to my cry for help -- I just assumed he was dead.

Some people came by. There was Larry Galindo, who had been in Beirut working with Catholic Services for a few months. He came by and he leaned over my face, looked me in the eye, and said, "I know Anne you're all right. I'm going to call or cable CRS, let them know that you're all right." That made me feel good, because I thought some people might think I was dead. Another time, Jamous, who worked with USAID, came and recognized me. But somebody, a Lebanese, whom I knew and who knew me, came and stood over me and just looked at me and looked at me but didn't say my name or anything. And it was really hard for me to talk. So I couldn't say anything like, you know, "My name is Anne Dammarell; call my family." I couldn't do that. I just thought it was strange. He had a blank look, with no human response. Now, my guess is he probably was somebody from the embassy trying to identify people.

Then later in the day -- mind you, I was not in pain -- somebody, a nurse I guess, gave me a bag of glucose and stuck it in my arm. She taped the bag on the wall. After a little bit the tape fell off and the bag fell and pulled the needle out of my arm, but not completely. So that's the pain I had for a couple of hours; that was my only pain. Then Tish Butler came by, and I think Jill Mandel was with her. Once again I felt assured that everything was going to be all right.

I think it was about 5:00 in the evening, and why I say that I don't know, but at some point somebody came and took me into a room and tried to put those great big black things, the X-ray film, under my back and that was *un*bearable. I was in great pain; every part of my body hurt. I yelled. I guess they took pictures, I don't know. They left. And I was still on this skinny little gurney and someone moved me in to a room. There was another woman there, a Lebanese woman, who could not speak English. I think she had been scheduled for surgery. They left me. I remember wanting to get a painkiller. So I called out.

"Hakim" was the only thing I could think of -- doctor, hakim. Finally, the Lebanese woman got out of her bed and walked down to get a nurse. A nurse, or somebody, came in and said to me, "We can't give you any medicine, because you had a concussion." I was there it seemed for an eternity. Diane Dillard came in late at night. I couldn't see her, because I couldn't move my neck.

*Q: I've interviewed Diane.*

DAMMARELL: Oh, you have?

*Q: She was in the consular section when I was consul general in Athens, earlier.*

DAMMARELL: Ah, she was a brick; she was solid throughout this. I can just see her taking charge, because she's a very calm person by nature. She came in. She and I were friends. She came in with Philo Dibble and introduced me to Philo. I don't remember him saying anything. She said he had just come. That cracked me up and I began to laugh, because I thought, "On your first day and you walk into something like this?" I laughed and it hurt. So I tried to stop myself from laughing. She told me that Bill McIntyre had been killed. Bill and I had worked together. He had been brought in as AID rep when Peter Cody left. Then they brought in Malcolm Butler to expand the AID mission and Bill was his deputy. So I knew Bill was dead. I asked Diane to call a friend of mine who was in Rome, because I had already planned to stop off in Rome before going home. I wanted Diane to let him know that I wouldn't be there. I was due to leave Beirut the next week. She said, yes, she would take care of that and I felt relief. I didn't understand the magnitude of anything really, for a long time I didn't get it.

*Q: What happened to the people who were in the cafeteria with you?*

DAMMARELL: Bob and I were the only two in the cafeteria that lived. The awful part is they all died. You know, people talk about feeling guilt. I never felt guilty. I just felt terrible. I felt bad that they died and I didn't die. I always felt extraordinarily happy about being alive. I had a sense of joy that I had never experienced before. It was a total awareness that life is a gift. I understood that. I was very happy. That lasted for almost a year. It wasn't just a temporary thing. I wish I still had it. I don't. But for a year practically nothing bothered me, because I was alive. But there were a lot of people who were not. There were fourteen Americans who were killed in that bombing, the total was sixty-three people. There were a large number of Lebanese employees, staff. State lost a lot. There was a CIA meeting, and they lost some of the best. Bob Ames was one of them, head of the Middle East area. And AID lost too. So on the whole, it was bad. There were some people, some Lebanese, who were standing in line to get a visa or were just walking on the Corniche and they got caught up in it.

I was lucky to get a room in the hospital, because a lot of the people were operated on in the corridors and other sections. Before they put me in a bed at night, they had to cut off my shirt. They didn't set any of my bones, but they wrapped my arms in splints, so they got bundled. They cut off my clothes. I was essentially naked. I didn't have a sheet on me. They were trying to clean my left leg that had a great big gash in it and that hurt. So I once again was asking for painkillers, and they said, "No, no, we can't give you any." Then a door opened; there was a swinging door. I wasn't alone. There were other people in this room and doctors were working on other people.

The door opened and it was Father Campbell, who was a Jesuit friend at St. Joseph University. I saw him and heard him call out, "Anne Dammarell? Is Anne Dammarell here?" I said yes. I guess I was talking by that time. When he approached, I thought I was making a joke when I said, "I want extreme unction," which is, as you know, the anointing of the dead. He said, "That's why I'm here." And I was *shocked*. He did anoint me. He put oil on my head and said a little prayer and then he turned and left. I felt a little embarrassed because I looked a mess. I had no idea what I looked like, but I presumed I looked a mess. Then the next thing I knew, Morrie Draper's wife came in. Do you remember her?

*Q: I know Morrie Draper.*

DAMMARELL: Yes. He and his wife came in. I met her before I left for Beirut, because she's a friend of a friend of mine. She came in and she was perfectly attired and her hair was coiffed and I could smell her perfume. And she said, "Who do you want me to call?" Well, I couldn't think of any names or numbers or anything. So I said, "No, no, everything's all right. Everything's all right." When I looked up and saw Morrie, he looked away, and then they left.

They stitched me up. They stitched my leg up. I think it was at that time somebody came up to me and asked if a woman not far away from me was Mary Lee McIntyre. Well, I couldn't see. I heard, "Wake up." So I knew some woman -- well, I knew it was a woman because they asked me if that was Mary Lee McIntyre -- was being wakened up after surgery, to see if she was coming out of the anesthesia. I don't know what I said, but there was no way I could identify her.

So I'm in bed the next day -- this is Tuesday. I don't know who organized this, but the women associated with the embassy or Lebanese who were married to Americans or who worked at the embassy began a shift. I'm assuming they did it for other people. They would come into my room on four-hour shifts or perhaps a couple-hour shifts. I had somebody in my room all the time and they helped me. They would feed me or give me a bedpan. Nobody tried to wash me. It was interesting, because some people have something in their personality or in their physical being that when they're in the room with you you're very calm.

Other people make you anxious, or made me anxious. It had nothing to do with what they said or did; it was just their being there, and you absorbed that. I think you absorb fear. There were two young women, Maura Hart was one, and an Italian named Maria. They were just super. They came in and they tried to help me. I kept saying, "I'm in pain." Maura -- I mean they were young, they were in mid-twenties, I think -- Maura said, "Well, just relax and breathe out. Push out the pain." You know, it helped me. They helped me focus. Now, the pain was still there, but it gave me something to do. It gave me some sort of control over my body.

Dr. Pettigrew came in, from Cairo I believe. They couldn't do my surgery. They had scheduled surgery the next day and that got postponed, and actually it got postponed the next day too. There was just so much work that mine was more or less elective surgery compared to what they were dealing with. He asked me if I wanted to go to Germany. I said no. I was very vehement. I did not want to go to Germany. I didn't bother to tell him what my fear was. My fear was I didn't know anybody in Germany and I didn't speak German. It was totally irrational.

Q: *Well, it made sense. I mean you were with family.*

DAMMARELL: Yes, that's right. And I trusted the medical care at AUB.

At one point Bob Pearson came in. Maybe this was on the third day. He was in the hospital. He had had shrapnel removed that had been near his eye. He was wrapped in a sheet. He came to tell me, to see how I was. Actually he said, "Anne, I came to tell you I love you." When you hear that outside of this context it sounds phony. But when you think you're dying, that's what you want to tell people, that you love them. That's paramount. He had seen Mary Lee. Mary Lee had an eye injury. I think she had a piece of glass in her eye. That's what they were operating on. Her cousin was going to come meet her. Bob knew I had sisters. He said, "You should ask one of your sisters to come." And I thought, "Oh yes, that's a good idea." So I asked that Elizabeth come. and somebody from the embassy came and said, "Oh, we can't authorize that." I said, "Well, I'll pay for it," because I really wanted somebody. I wanted my family. Actually the government did pay for her ticket.

I'd forgotten this. The very first night when I was in AUB hospital somebody came in with a phone. Now, this was before cell phones. I don't know how they got an extension cord. It was my sister Alice. She said, "Anne, I've seen you on television and you look *beautiful.*" I talked to her. At the time I didn't quite believe her. I knew she wasn't hallucinating, but I thought well, she's just making this up to make me feel good. That was basically the extent of the conversation. And you know, she was right, they had a clip on ABC of me being taken out of the embassy. She had seen that and recognized me. How that happened, I don't know. I didn't make that up; that really did happen.

But, getting back to AUB, they didn't have visiting hours. It seemed everybody I knew came in and visited me. A lot of Lebanese were there. They'd come in and look at me and leave. I remember seeing Ryan and Christine at the foot of the bed. I woke up and they were standing there and I talked to them, I *think* I talked to them. I believe people came to see me because everybody was so concerned about the embassy being bombed and they wanted to be in contact with somebody. I was the one that was in the hospital, and they knew me; so that's why. But I got really tired. So when Dr. Pettigrew came again I said, "Yes, I will go to Germany," thinking I just need to get this over with, I need to be taken care of.

The CIA sent in a plane for one of their staff that had not been killed but was injured. He was in that meeting but had left to go to the john. He was there when the explosion took place and he fell down a flight, he pivoted down, and broke his ankle. I don't think he ever was unconscious. They brought in a plane on Friday and the people at the hospital gave me something so I could have a more peaceful flight. It was a barbiturate of some sort. I did dose off and I hallucinated. I was a pink airplane and I was flying in the sky *(laughs)* and every time I'd see a building I'd try to land. I'd get down there and I'd zoom up again. Oh, I woke up exhausted. That morning the Army or Air Force came. There were two women, medical women, nurses. They were just wonderful, because they could pick me up and put me on another gurney and I was pain-free.

*Q: They had medical teams that did this sort of thing. My wife was evacuated once from Yugoslavia.*

DAMMARELL: Well, they're pros and, you know, when they handle you, you don't feel pain. When I was in the hospital, if somebody would touch just one part of my body, my whole body hurt. It wasn't just my arm; everything hurt. So I didn't want anybody near me. I was real tense when people would come towards me. But it was wonderful with these women. The inside of the plane was covered in baby blue carpeting throughout. The walls had baby blue carpeting. I had a doctor there who examined me. I don't remember what he did. I don't think he gave me any medicine. We flew to Wiesbaden, and there was of course an ambulance that took us to the hospital. A nurse, a woman, cleaned me up. What she was doing was removing the gunk that was on my body. I still have a little bit of the stuff. It's black, like tar. They're called tattoo scars. Before she started, a doctor came in, and his name was Wiedemann. Is that the name of the beer? Because I remember I associate it with beer. He said, "I will examine you. But first of all you have to be cleaned up," and that's when the nurse came in. And she did it very gently. She was there for a long time. When finished, she asked if I would like something to eat. I said, "Yes, I'm hungry. I want a chef salad." She said, "It's midnight and I don't know if we can open up the kitchen or not, but I'll see what I can do for you." She did bring me a chef salad.

The next day the doctor examined me. He said, "I can do the work here, but you'll have to stay here through the physical therapy as well as the surgery." And he said, "That'll be a long time. You stay here *or* if you want me to, I can authorize you to be flown back to the States." And I said, "Oh, send me back to the States, because I want to be near family." I also asked to be sent to Washington, because that was my home. That was where I wanted to go. Also, I knew nurses and doctors in Washington and I thought that would help me. So he did do that. He, he said, "When you're stable we'll send you back." I don't know what stable meant. I have *notoriously* low blood pressure, which always worries medical doctors. So they might have been thinking of my blood pressure.

I bet I was there towards the very end of April. Because by the time I was flown to Washington -- and the operation was like the day after I got there -- it was May 1. They operated on my arm. I had a fabulous doctor, George Bogomil, who had been in the army. He was really the top of the line. I had excellent care. He told me that he was going to do my left arm and put a steel plate in it, and that he was not going to operate on my right arm. He was going to just kind of squish it together and put it in a cast. There were breaks there, but it didn't require surgery. And he did that. I had other things that had to be done, like my fingers were broken and they had to be reset, and it turned out my foot was broken in several places. Bogomil said he wanted to put off additional surgeries until the next summer.

I had to learn to walk again. I had forgotten how to walk. That was one thing I had to learn to do. I had to build up strength. Something must have hit me on the left side, because my shoulder was broken and the scapula was broken and dislodged, and all my ribs on the left side were broken. My fingers were broken and it was my left foot that was broken, a big cut on my left leg. So it was mainly my left side that got whacked. And I didn't have any strength.

So strange -- I had to learn how to sit up and to turn over. I guess my brain was scrambled, that's the only thing I can think of. I remember they brought me a food menu and asked me to choose something. I had a pen and when I wrote it wasn't cursive writing. I had to write it in print because I had forgotten. I wasn't conscious of it, but I had forgotten how to do cursive. And that's when it really got to me and I began to cry, because I thought, "I'm back in kindergarten." You know, I had to print block letters with my broken arm. Also, it hurt.

Now, this is totally normal for somebody who's been in some sort of trauma. I heard a loud bang, somebody must have dropped something outside the window. I don't know what it was. It made a noise. I rang for the nurse and told her that I had to be moved away from the window because there was a bomb that had just gone off and that she couldn't be near windows, otherwise she'd get cut. I was informing her. She didn't respond in any particular way. I guess she thought I was hallucinating. But she didn't contradict me either. Which is probably good. When I was in the hospital, the routine was in the morning I'd have physical therapy and in -- at that time, maybe it's still this way -- a very big room with other patients. At first they put me in a little room off the big room and the physical therapists examined me and determined what they were going to do for me. Then they put me in the big room. They had bars for me to put my hands on while I walked and I cross-walked, like this. And then eventually they had exercises, strength-building exercises. But the good of that was this: as immobile as I was, I still knew I was getting better, I knew I was healthy. I knew that. And I never thought that I wouldn't get back to being normal. There's an intense desire to be normal, and that didn't leave me for years. You just want everything to be the way it was. But I would see people coming in who were in real serious conditions. So I never felt like "poor me," because I knew I was better off than most people. And it's not a Pollyanna attitude. It's simply a realization that I was better off than others.

And then of course I had family and they all came. They flew in from Ohio and New York and they would visit and they'd go back. I really couldn't be with visitors. I really couldn't. The nurses didn't let them in, and it was a good thing, because I needed a lot of sleep. I needed a tremendous amount of sleep, and with people there you don't get it. I do though remember, and I was grateful he came, Bob Pugh visited. Bob Pugh was the DCM and he was in DC while I was in the hospital. I was eager to find out what had happened, who was killed, how serious was it. I wanted all the details. The hospital staff was trying to protect me from getting this information. I found that a little annoying. So when Bob came he told me what he knew. It was a bomb. I think it was he who said it was two thousand pounds of dynamite.

*Q: What did you know and later hear? I mean, what happened? For somebody reading this, I mean they might have read other accounts, but what did you hear?*

DAMMARELL: At that point I knew very little. It was Bob who told me that a truck filled with dynamite had been near the Corniche and had been given a signal to go up to the embassy itself. The embassy had an apron driveway and there were guards at either end. But instead of driving in the way you should drive in, the truck drove down and entered the back way and it went straight into the driveway and ran into the front door of the embassy. When it blew, the building imploded and that whole section of the embassy, that section at the front door, pancaked down. You'll see pictures of the floors. That was Post One, as a matter fact. That was when Bobby McMaugh, who was our marine on duty, was killed. Anybody in that section died. And that section is where the CIA was having their meeting, that's why so many of their staff members were killed. Right next to front door, immediately next to it, was the cafeteria. I suspect the people who were right there were evaporated. Others had various other kinds of wounds and died.

Most of the staff, I think, stayed in Beirut after the bombing. I think some people were allowed to come home on TDY. I know Diane Dillard came back sometime that summer, because she visited me when I was out of the hospital.

The bombing was significant because it was the first time they had a suicide bomber go in and hit the embassy. We had had our ambassador, who was there several years beforehand, kidnapped and killed. Other people had been targeted as individuals, but this was the embassy itself. And you know, it's history now. The embassies are now so protected, they're referred to as fortresses. It wasn't that way when I was initially in the service.

# RECOVERY AND SRI LANKA

I was at the hospital until about the end of June. Dr. Bogomil said I needed to have extended therapy, but he wasn't going to do any more operations. He was going to put me in a nursing home. And I thought, "Oh my God, I don't want to be in a nursing home." I asked if I couldn't make arrangements. I had a couple of nieces in Cincinnati, Annie and Kathy, who were seniors, graduating from college that summer. And then Tara came from New York. I asked if they would come and live with me. I rented a house of a friend of mine who goes to Spain every year. So they came. I was an outpatient. I would go into the hospital and do my exercises every day. It was like a job. I did that most of the summer. I was in a wheelchair originally, but I eventually got out of that and was able to walk with a walker, and then they gave me crutches, and then I just walked on my own.

Actually this happened even when I was in Wiesbaden -- as I said earlier, I was happy. I was aware people were dead and I wanted to mourn. I felt like I should be mourning, I should be unhappy about their deaths. But I was just bubbling over with life. I asked to see a psychiatrist, because I thought this was not normal. So I asked to see a psychiatrist, and when I was in Wiesbaden a psychiatrist came, he was Indian. He said that the best thing to do was just to focus on healing and getting my bones together and not to think of anything, that that would come in time, I would be able to process that in time.

He asked if I had any religious orientation, and I said, yes, I'd been raised a Roman Catholic. And he said, "Well, in time you'll have some sort of reaction that will be like a spiritual process." Then he left. My sister Elizabeth had flown to Wiesbaden and I told her about it and I said, "That's totally useless, that's not helping me at all, I mean that's useless information." Well, of course, he was right. Because when I say it was like a job -- it is. If you have to get better, that's what you have to focus on, with all your energy and that's it. Then a psychiatrist, a State Department psychiatrist, came to see me at the hospital in DC and suggested that I might not be able to go to my post in Sri Lanka. That triggered a reaction right away. Because when I said I wanted to be normal, to be normal to me at that point was to go to the onward assignment. And actually, Sarah Jane Littlefield, who was the director out there, held it for me, which was very nice of her. So I did get to go there and that made me feel a little bit normal.

I did ask to see a psychiatrist while at Georgetown Hospital. I never had been to a psychiatrist before, and I had heard it was a very lengthy process. I didn't want to make it longer by miscommunication. So I asked that I see a woman and a Roman Catholic, and possibly someone of Irish descent. Because I figured if there's any cultural bias then we'll be on the same playing field. Well, I got all those things. And Margaret Clancy was wonderful. Analysis was completely different from what I expected. I thought they'd give me some advice, because one of the things I went to see her about were my nightmares. When I was in the house where I was living and sleeping I would get nightmares. This happened for a while. They weren't just in Washington; they would come back while in Sri Lanka.

These nightmares were not of the Beirut bombing, but in every dream I was in a foreign country and I was in danger. I mean in danger like I was being shot at or I was walking across a bridge and the bridge began to fall down, or at one point I was walking into an elevator and it wasn't there and I fell down the shaft. In my dream I was dead and I knew that was scary. So that was what motivated me to see Margaret Clancy. It did help, because after a while the dreams stopped. One of the things she said to do was talk about the bombing. I had been reluctant to talk about the bombing to some degree. If anybody asked me a question I'd answer it, but it was -- as Tish Butler said at one point when I interviewed her later on, years later, "There's a two-minute response and there's a two-hour response, and people only want that two-minute response." People ask about it, but they really don't want to hear about it. Most people can't listen to all that stuff. It's not interesting. I remember that was one of the things that I thought -- that I should be more open about this. I eventually got to a point where I was all right. I was well enough.

I went to Sri Lanka in January 1984. When I went to the embassy -- AID was not in the embassy, like we had been in Beirut -- and saw that the only security they had was a big thick chain with a padlock across the gate, I thought, "Oh my goodness, that's not much security." But things were calm at the beginning of my tour. Then the Tamil Tigers started up again. They would rob banks. They'd steal dynamite from project sites, all the things that had gone on in Beirut. I remember going to Frank Correll, who was the director, and saying, "Well, it's going to start up again. We have to have somebody in the north, because if civil war breaks out we have to have contacts there and we have to know the community there." He didn't, of course, take my advice. I went home that summer for my hand surgery and for my foot surgery the following summer.

While in Sri Lanka there was a bombing in a hotel near the embassy. I was having lunch when the bomb went off and said to the people with me, "That was a bomb." No one said anything and we continued to eat. I guess they didn't believe me. It actually was a bomb. Things heated up. Killings started in earnest. I remember being aware of it. I don't know that I was so much afraid or, if I was, I wasn't telling myself I was afraid. Then there was a kidnapping of some contractors. I think three people were kidnapped. That really set off the alarm inside my head and I couldn't sleep. The nightmares started again and I thought, "Uh-uh, I just can't function." I understood that nobody could protect me and I thought something was going to happen and it wasn't going to be good. So instead of having the two tours -- AID had a system where you would go out for two two-year tours -- I stayed only three years and came back to Washington. I was then forty-nine, and since you can retire at fifty in the Foreign Service, I did. I worked in evaluation for a while and then retired.

*Q: Let's talk a little bit more about Sri Lanka. What was the situation like when you were there?*

DAMMARELL: In the beginning it wasn't bad, but there was a civil war going on. The Tamil Tigers were organizing. Travel was restricted. It got to a point where you didn't go north into Tamil territory. I did not think we were going to be bombed, but I had a very strong reaction to the kidnapping of those contractors. That frightened the hell out of me. But, no, it was nothing like Beirut, where you saw militia with guns all over the place and car bombings. It wasn't like that. There was a war going on, but to me it seemed very distant.

*Q: What were they doing there?*

DAMMARELL: AID had mainly agriculture and water projects.

*Q: Were you finding things, AID-wise, going along pretty well?*

DAMMARELL: Yes, it's a beautiful country. I think people who like the outdoors would love it because there's a lot to do, a lot of activities, water, sports, and hiking, and bird watching. Buddhist and Hindu, the two cultures are there. It was a small post; people were very friendly; AID worked closely with the embassy. If I remember correctly, there were a lot of young people posted there. I'd never been to the tropics before, so I found that interesting.

*Q: Who was the ambassador?*

DAMMARELL: I can't remember his name. He was a political appointee.

*Q: Yes. It's often a political appointee.*

DAMMARELL: Is that right?

*Q: Yes. Man who was governor of Maine was there twice.*

DAMMARELL: Yes. Well, if you like the outdoors it would really be a wonderful posting.

*Q: After your horrendous experiences in Beirut, did you find you ever carried a grudge or animosity towards the powers that be, or powers that were?*

DAMMARELL: No, I didn't. I've read -- and people would tell me -- you'll get angry at God. I never got angry at God. I didn't get angry at the government. I didn't get angry at AID. I didn't get angry, even, at the bomber. I thought, "You poor bastard." I just made up a whole scenario. He was disenfranchised, he was stupid, he never had a chance, and he was hoodwinked. I had no idea that suicide bombers would be thought of as heroes. That never entered my head. When I found out -- somebody told me, and I don't even know if it was true -- the man who signaled the bomber was a friendly Palestinian I knew, I felt sad, not angry. Later when I found out that Iran had sponsored the bombing, I wanted Iran to be held publicly responsible, which is why I sued. Some believe the terrorists were after the CIA and not the ambassador. It would seem logical that they wanted to wipe out the CIA.

*Q: But they wouldn't know, I mean you don't know when meetings are...*

DAMMARELL: Yes, that's right. The reason Ambassador Dillon didn't get killed was that he was called away. Somebody had phoned him and he felt like he had to answer the call. He went back to his office and was putting on a sweatshirt because he was going to go out for a run. Because he had done that, he was not in the elevator. His secretary had alerted the marines at Post One, also the drivers, that he was on his way down. When that happens the drivers start up the cars and get ready. So he was supposed to be in that elevator, but he wasn't there. You know Bob Dillon.

*Q: Yes. Bob and I are both in the same retirement home. I've interviewed Bob.*

DAMMARELL: I think that's why the embassy was targeted, to get him.

# LIFE AFTER THE
# FOREIGN SERVICE

*Q: So you retired when?*

DAMMARELL: 1988.

*Q: What have you been doing since?*

DAMMARELL: Well, first of all, fifty's too young for retirement, way too young. Shortly after retirement, a friend -- one of the Maryknoll brothers studying Arabic in Beirut -- called and asked me to teach English in Egypt during the summer. He had set up a program for the seminarians at the Coptic Catholic Seminary and was starting an English program in Alexandria, so that the seminarians -- most of them were from Upper Egypt and had not traveled -- could have some idea of what it was like to be on a beach. I went and it was a wonderful experience; loved it. The Coptic Catholic Seminary had been started by two Jesuits, one from Holland and one from Malta. The priest from Holland asked me to stay, but I really wanted to go home to start my life. After I got home I thought, "What am I doing?" I returned for a year and stayed for three. I liked the Egyptians quite a bit. When the first Iraq War started I thought it unwise for me to be in Cairo. I thought that there would be a bombing of the American University or the embassy.

I returned to DC and began to volunteer for Rhonda Buckley. She was starting a center for the arts for neighborhood children in the basement of Jubilee Housing, a housing project in Adams Morgan. She had been an elementary teacher and a musician. She wanted to establish a safe environment for the children to go after school and before their parents came home. The center opened up primarily with music classes and expanded. Both the child and the parent had to agree that the child would come to class and practice fifteen minutes a day. I taught the children creative writing, and some of the Latina mothers English. Eventually Rhonda raised enough money to build the Sitar Center for the Arts in Adams Morgan. She liaised with the Levine School of Music, the National Symphony, Arena Stage, Septime Webre's Washington Ballet, and others. All the teachers are volunteers.

After a while I got a master's focusing on Middle Eastern studies at Georgetown University. I wanted my thesis to be on the bombing of the embassy. I still didn't know who bombed us. To my surprise little had been written on the embassy, but there was a tremendous amount on the Marine bombing in October 1983. They lost 241 men in that suicide bombing. There were magazines, books, and psychiatrists' articles. That's when I read about post-traumatic stress. I didn't understand that I had experienced PTSD (post-traumatic stress disorder) myself. I knew the dreams gave me a terrible time. I understood they were because of the bombing. I just couldn't make them stop.

There were other things that I understood were related to the bombing, but I couldn't control them. For instance, if I flew, whenever I got in line I'd look at people around me to see, "Is somebody here carrying a bomb?" That was a routine thing. I went in the post office once and saw a package just sitting there. I went up to the clerk and told him that he had to call the police, that they had to look at that. They thought I was crazy.

But all of these are normal reactions if you've been in something like Beirut. I read about PTSD and I thought, "Oh my God, that's what happened to me." And I felt relief. I was normal. After reading interviews of marines and their reactions, I thought, "Well, I would like to know what our people thought." So I decided that for my thesis I would interview people who were in the embassy at the time and get their reaction to that day. I also had them fill out a questionnaire. The questionnaire was anonymous and related to the classic symptoms of PTSD. I mailed that out to anybody I had an address for. I only talked to the people who were here in Washington; either they were posted here or they lived here. I talked to a number of people and I loved it. I had been reluctant to talk to people, because you never know; sometimes you just don't know what kind of response you're going to get.

*Q: Oh yes.*

DAMMARELL: You probably know better than most people because of what you do. I learned a lot. I learned that a lot of people had reactions that were similar to my own reaction. I learned that they got together. They were lucky to have Bob Pugh and Bob Dillon, because both of those men had military experience and, you know, the military does prepare you for things like this. They met every day to talk. It wasn't just a staff meeting. It was, I suppose, *a* staff meeting, trying to figure out what you're going to do at the embassy, but they had the whole community there. They could express their pros and cons. It turns out that some people, if you mention the word psychiatrist, climb the wall. The idea was abhorrent -- to talk to a psychiatrist. Some people were cynical. Some just didn't like the idea. Others did and were open to it. I think there was an attitude of "you have to have been there to know what it was like." You really just can't talk to anybody.

You really have to have some knowledge of what it's like. Now, Margaret Clancy had never been in a bombing and I did find it very helpful to talk to her. So that just disproves what I said. But I did think, and I still feel that way, that it's kind of like how the marines are so tight because they were in a war together. There was a certain unspoken understanding among those who were in the bombing together. You might feel that way about the air force and your experience with Korea. That's an attitude I heard expressed by several Foreign Service officers I interviewed. They were lucky to have had one another. One of the things that Faith Lee said really resonated with me mainly because of my dreams. She had gone on to her onward posting; I think it was Japan. But she had a yearning to go back to Beirut. She did return on TDY (temporary duty) and afterwards was at peace. My colleagues were really good. They were nice to talk to me and I'm glad that I interviewed them. It was good; it was very good for me.

*Q: You wrote it up?*

DAMMARELL: I did.

*Q: Were you able to get any distribution, for example to the medical side of the State Department?*

DAMMARELL: Diane Dillard did that. Everybody that was interviewed got a copy of the thesis, including the medical department. I have no idea if it had any impact on anybody or not.

*Q: If a lot of copies were distributed, it probably ended up somewhere.*

DAMMARELL: Well I talked to people in State Med, so I know they had gotten a copy. Beirut was the beginning. After Kenya and Tanzania in East Africa had their embassies bombed, the survivors were very vocal and they wanted a meeting. State Med -- the psychiatrists -- helped out with their meeting. I think the meeting was probably a very good idea; they had a chance to talk.

*Q: Tell me about the Dammarell versus Islamic Republic of Iran lawsuit you referred to earlier.*

DAMMARELL: The Foreign Sovereign Immunities Act was amended in 1996 to allow a ten-year time period for U.S. citizens who were injured overseas to sue seven countries that sponsored terrorism, or for a suit to be brought on behalf of those who were killed. Iran was one of the seven countries listed.

Terry Anderson's case was big news. He won a judgment against Iran in 2000, proving that Hezbollah was linked to Iran and that both were responsible for his kidnapping in Beirut in 1985. When my sister Elizabeth asked why I hadn't sued, I told her I had been in the Foreign Service and was not eligible. Her advice to me was, "Check it out." I did. I phoned Anderson's law firm, Crowell-Moring, and talked to Stu Newberger, who said that federal employees could indeed sue.

Our complaint wasn't filed until October 2001, because it took a long time to contact the families of the seventeen Americans killed and all those in the embassy at the time of the bombing to determine who wanted to be a plaintiff. Eighty-three victims or their families joined the suit.

On December 15, 2001, the U.S. District Court for the District of Columbia ruled that Iran supported Hezbollah terrorists in the April 18, 1983 bombing of the embassy. The plaintiffs have not yet collected any money from the judgment, but this lawsuit gave us a means of holding Iran publicly accountable for the bombing.

For years I hadn't known who was responsible, which was unsettling. I had originally expected to find out during the trial who had actually planned the bombing. We didn't, but we were able to prove Iran funded the project.

*The Good Spy: the Life and Death of Robert Ames* by Kai Bird came out on May 21, 2014. It is about the top CIA specialist on the Middle East, who was killed in the Beirut embassy bombing. Bird makes a case that Ali Reza Asgari, an Iranian who helped form Hezbollah in Lebanon, planned and supervised the 1983 bombings of the embassy and the Marine barracks and that, in exchange for information on Iran's nuclear power program, Asgari defected and sought asylum in the United States in 2007.

*Q: And so today what are you up to?*

DAMMARELL: Well, I do some volunteer teaching in Bangkok. I teach at a Buddhist monastery for about three months a year. I help out at the Sitar Center. And I walk a dog every morning. So there you go.

www.ingramcontent.com/pod-product-compliance
Lightning Source LLC
Chambersburg PA
CBHW071539120626

46550CB00006B/2506